Life is Short/ Death is Forever

*"Finding joy and pleasure in each day,
without hurting anyone along the way"*

STEVE A. HARTMAN, PH.D.

ISBN 13: 9781793898302

To my parents, Norman and Ethel, who gave me this incredible thing we call life, and to Ronnie, Josh, and the rest of my family, friends, and acquaintances, who enriched and continue to enrich my amazing experience on this beautiful planet Earth.

TABLE OF CONTENTS

PREFACE

This book is my look at life through the lens of my personal experiences and thoughts. I hope it provides you with what I like to find in the many books I choose to read: new information, a few challenging questions, and a little humor. Some will strongly disagree with my ideas and observations, others may find they resonate in their own lives, still others might discover insights that never occurred to them during their life's journey.

While seeking pleasure is what I truly believe drives us, it is not just seeking sensual pleasure and the avoidance of pain or suffering, which is the most limited definition of hedonism. I believe pleasure can be derived through the success of various human endeavors and accomplishments. Achieving pleasure, for me, is not the highest good, as a hedonist might believe. Most importantly it is not a personal selfish goal to be attained at the cost or harm of any other person.

Everyone has an interesting life story to tell. That's what makes it so exciting for me to meet and spend time with as many people as I can; it enriches my life. Every group meeting, get-together, socializing event with new people, taking courses with strangers, all create opportunities to meet someone who will be a friend for the rest of my life.

Each chapter can stand alone though reading it in the sequence the chapters are presented captures earlier events sometimes adding meaning because that's how it was written. Some of my experiences and insights are often built upon experiences, references, information, comments or conclusions from prior chapters.

The statistics, percentages, and other details have been carefully researched. I've chosen not to slow down the read with multiple footnotes. Any questionable numbers, percentages or references can be easily and quickly confirmed. In many cases these represent what is true as I write this book and are subject to change over time.

PROLOGUE

This is a collection of several essays, on various subjects, sharing observations, thoughts, and questions I've had during my life. Eternity is personal; to me it's my entire life and nothing that follows. While I have memories of many childhood experiences, my life as me, I feel began once I left home for my freshman year at college. It will end upon my death. Others may define their lives differently, but for me, all that matters happens during this time. Learning about lives that came before me is interesting – many provide vicarious lessons and inspiration – but these are not part of my real existence.

I believe we each have an expiration date built into our genetics. If not shortened by an accident or illness, our eternal lives will come to their predestined ends. We may each only have a set number of heartbeats, breaths, laughs and orgasms remaining. Where are the meaningful adult "Fortune Cookies" that might read, "A passionate life lies before you, enjoy another 500 orgasms in your future"? Would this mean making love more often will result in a shorter life, or stretching them out will result in a longer one? But what if a "Fortune Cookie" writer has a bad day? Might he write , "…enjoy eight more orgasms in your future?" This would be read as good news for someone in their late nineties, but not such good news if you're in your thirties. I dare say, if you are reading this book, then I have finished it before an accident, illness, or my expiration date arrived.

Not knowing when this will occur makes me want to enjoy every day. I love to take in all the colors, sights, sounds and textures of life around me. I want to provide positivity whenever possible toward my family, those people I care about, and those I meet along the way. I've made good decisions and others that were not so good, but I think being human requires us to be far less than perfect. In these pages I share both.

If a biological test can identify your expiration date, would you want to know?... I would. Not to do something crazy without consequences, but to soak up as much of life as I can before the end. Maybe to do things that might otherwise be embarrassing or somewhat risky. While taking such risks, I'd reach out for additional pleasure and enjoyment, but certainly not at anyone else's cost. While I don't know this final date, I'm still driven to push my inhibitions aside, as best I can with strangers, and even more so with people I know and can trust.

Along the way, I think laughing is one of the greatest gifts of life, after the pleasure of mutually consensual sex. Watch funny TV shows and films, read funny things, and laugh with friends as much as you can. At the end of each chapter, the best I can offer you of these two gifts of life, within these pages, is the gift of laughter, or at least a smile, with jokes or anecdotes that have made me laugh.

1

DEATH: THE FINISH LINE OF LIFE

We are each born with a death sentence. In fifty years most people alive today will be gone, in a hundred years just about everybody alive today will be dead. Yes, there will be some hangers-on who live past a hundred, but in our Human Race, we all eventually cross that finish line: death. This is one race where most of us want to be last among our friends, especially if we can do it in good health. A hundred years is about the best we can expect. If we reach this lofty goal in good health, it will be a wonderful life, but only a momentary blink in time. I've read that babies born today will have an average lifespan of about 103 years.

Contrary to this reality, I want this to be an uplifting book of thoughts and suggestions on getting the most out of the very short time any of us have. Our quality of life is not dependent on making lots of money, being famous, or having the highest level of education. If so, there wouldn't be so many very poor, anonymous, less educated people around the world without these things, and yet are very happy. Go figure!

In the best scenario, we don't even have a hundred years, making every year we do have so precious. And we can't buy back lost time, or save time in an account, withdrawing it as needed. I think we have little or no control over our lives until we reach eighteen or twenty; after leaving home, and sometimes, not even until some years later. We will sleep about one-third of our lives, so it too should be as pleasurable as possible. From our hundred years, subtract about thirty-three years for sleep, and a minimum of another seventeen years until we take control and responsibility for our own lives. This leaves us about forty or fifty years of living the lives we choose, or that choose us, with the people we meet, hopefully getting to do a lot of what we want to do in life.

Some of us cross that finish line when we're young, while others will be older. It's the one experience we will all have, yet we'll never be able to share it with anyone else. Ideally, death will come to us as a surprise, only those around us will know we have died. Strange to think we will be left out of this very important moment. It may come quickly as a sudden heart attack, aneurism, stroke or accident. No matter how much joy, laughter, and pleasure we have had in our lives, will it be enough, particularly if there could have been more? To me it's simple to know what death will be like, and if I described it, I'm sure you'd agree. There is no pain, depression, or anxiety in death, but there is also no joy, satisfaction and pleasure.

Our lives take convoluted paths from beginning to end, each one interesting and unique. My interest in meeting lots of people is more than the writer in me; maybe it's an innate hunger to maximize my own existence. I sometimes wonder if the paths we take are predestined, though I try to hold on to the tenet that each time I make a decision I take more control of my life. But do I?

My most powerful experience with death occurred in Italy, the year after I graduated from college. I was a senior in college when I decided to become a doctor. My grade average at SUNY, the State University of New York, was only a "B." I had no family who were doctors and my family could not fund a building at a U.S. med school. In addition, my mediocre grade on the MCAT, the Medical Admission Test, used by medical colleges to gauge whether a person was smart enough to endure the rigors of a medical education, killed my chances of being accepted to an American med school. But we have to go back four years earlier, to understand the little exuberance others had for my academic talents.

According to my high school guidance counselor, I was already rolling a boulder uphill by just trying to get into any college. She advised me to apply to a trade school, learn a skill, because in her opinion, I was not college material. But surprise, surprise! A college accepted me because I played soccer. I was by no measure a star, but I had what they wanted – a penis.

Several years before I was accepted, this college had transitioned from a fancy women's finishing school, so they needed to build up their population with testosterone-carrying students. They were short on men, even short men, and needed more males for their men's soccer, basketball, swimming, and tennis teams. I learned that year to never let anyone else set limits as to what I can or cannot do, even if my ultimate success, in this case, was the result of serendipity and luck. It's a process I like to call "putting myself in the way of life and getting run over whenever possible."

Back to death... That summer after college graduation, I met Stephen while installing a window air conditioner in his home. It was what I did for my summer job. He and another American had just lost their third roommate who graduated from the med school they attended in Italy. Stephen suggested I go to the Italian Embassy in Manhattan, apply for the fall term. I thought he was joking, it was already the beginning of August. Clearly he badly needed someone to share their three bedroom apartment in Bologna.

Stephen insisted there was enough time to apply and get in before classes started the end of September. What did I have to lose, except for the fact I was not Italian, did not know a word of Italian, and everything at this school was in Italian; no written exams, all exams were oral. I applied. As if by a Papal miracle, I was accepted. I paid $350 for the first year's tuition and was on the cruise ship Michelangelo heading for Italy four or five weeks after meeting Stephen.

I took Italian lessons on the ship; learned to count, find a bathroom, read a menu, follow Maria and Tony around their house and village in the simple book we used. Before unpacking the day I arrived, I signed up for lessons at Johns Hopkins extension, located in Bologna. They taught Italian in English. I was required the first day of classes to sign up and attend Italian lessons, in Italian, at the University of Bologna.

I did everything I could to learn Italian, including talking to our housekeeper, Alda. When I was home I followed her around the apartment. I sat in the kitchen talking with her as she prepared lunch. During dinner and sometimes lunch, I got to talk a little English with Stephen and Barry, my roommates. After lunch, more Italian with Alda as she did some light clean-ing. When I didn't have a class, I studied in my room while listening to the radio, which was all in Italian. The popular song then was "Down Town" by Petula Clark, which they sang in Italian as "Ciao, Ciao." I attended medical classes at the university using both American and Italian medical books alongside my most important book, the Italian/English dictionary.

I had wished I could master Italian at least as good as the five- and six-year-old children I saw every day on the street. But even that low bar was a reach. On many weekends I would travel with my friends on the "Setta Bella" (Beautiful Seven) train that went to Florence and Rome. It was this Fall, when I was there as a student, that the Arno river flooded Florence and washed millions of dollars of cameos, gold, silver and gems down the river from the Ponte Vecchio bridge. Cars floated down the streets of Florence smashing into many of the old buildings. The Uffizi Gallery had to move precious art from the ground floor and basement to above the water line.

A few weeks after classes began it was time for me to attend my first autopsy. I walked to the university under the porticos along the street, past the shopkeepers who wore their dark-colored aprons and work coats as they swept the sidewalks in front of their shops. It often rained, sometimes lightly snowed, in the late fall and winter, so the porticos helped. Many of the old buildings were red brick and plaster. The air was crisp and deli-cious with the aromas of food leaking out of the shops I passed. Each day I stopped for a cup of espresso and an Italian kiss. This candy kiss is like a Hershey's Kiss, also wrapped in a silver wrapper, except with the word "Bacio" in blue and a hazelnut in the center. So good! (Bacio means kiss in Italian.) They had to be unwrapped without the help of that little strip of tissue paper sticking out of the top of a Hershey's Kiss. There was no real top; they were rounded and inside was a love-note-saying printed on a clear piece of wax paper. Of course it was in Italian.

I am struck by the many people who have attended this school over the years. It is old, really old. How old? In fact, The University of Bologna is the oldest university in the world, established in 1088. Copernicus was a student here. The reddish stone buildings, of no more than three sto-ries, with wide hallways and high ceilings, house many of the rooms and amphitheater lecture halls, just as they were about nine hundred years ago. Yes, the furniture in the classrooms were updated. They couldn't have been more than a hundred years old.

The autopsy amphitheater, with wooden rails behind which students can observe the dissection for major anatomical presentations, seems to be original. The medical school was established a few years after the University, in 1200. It is the oldest medical school in the world. Some of Michelangelo's wood carvings of autopsies are on display in the medical library. Sadly, for Italians, there is always an "unhealthy" supply of cadavers, thus the medical school has no shortage of bodies for study.

White-haired, goateed Professor Benati meets with our anatomy lab class in a cold basement hallway; thousands of students before us must have gathered here. Professors are more highly regarded in Italy than doctors, so we dare not address him as Doctor Benati, a tip drilled into my head by my American roommates, both of whom are in their second year. Benati tells us, "If anyone feels ill, leave the room. If one of you faints, please, those around the falling student help prevent him or her from hitting the marble table or floor. If they do, and require medical attention, none of you are yet prepared to offer such attention." Though he is quite religious, he has a bit of a sense of humor. I so much do not want to be one of those students dropping to the floor.

The cadaver prep area is dark. A bright light, near the center of the room, hangs over a cold white marble table. The eight of us, four women and four men, file in, all wearing the requisite white lab coats. In those days there were an equal number of women and men in Italian medical schools, while in the U.S. there was probably less than one woman for every ten men.

A dark-haired woman, who looks older than her stated age of thirty-one, lies on her back, the table slightly elevated toward her head. She looks so peaceful, like she's sleeping, except she's naked and lying on a slab of cold marble. This is a first for me. Never before in my life has a naked woman not conjured thoughts of anticipation or sexual fantasy.

Our professor stands to her right; two students to his right and the rest of us crowd around the other three sides of the table. A female student stands behind her head, a guy by her feet, the other four of us along her left side. I am to the left of Angela, a pretty blonde. About one-quarter of the women in Northern Italy, to my surprise, are blonde. She stands to the left of the woman's head; I'm by her breasts, which are a bit flattened to her chest. Marcello, a comic in both Italian and English, is to my left.

The night before, Marcello had taken me to an Italian nightclub which was down some stairs beneath a store, not far from the railway station. Many of the guys and girls were Italian, but some were from the U.S. and various other countries. Marcello pointed out the many Italian girls who had been accompanied to this dancehall by aunts, chaperones of various types, including mothers. Marcello had no inhibitions when it came to women. He told me his philosophy as we walked to the dance club. "Stephano, a woman, she cannot ask to make love. It is the man who must ask, this gives the woman the chance to say yes." He was one of the happiest and funniest guys I met at med school that year. Back to our autopsy.

Darkness surrounds the bright, illuminated, naked and still body of this woman on the table, creating a respectful silence. The room is a little cold with a touch of damp basement smell. Benati tells us she died during childbirth, with her fourth child. He switches on a light over a table several feet away. We all turn to see her child, a boy, dwarfed by his white marble table. Benati rails about the terrible prenatal care afforded women in Italy at this time, which is little more than confirming pregnancy.

He reaches for a scalpel, holds it with his index finger on top of its spine. He looks around to make eye contact with each of us, then says, "Love the people God gave you, because one day he'll take them back."

He slides his left gloved hand down her chest, between her breasts, to locate the xiphoid process, the bottom of her sternum (breastbone), and then places the scalpel, held in his right hand below it with the blade facing down toward her navel. He hesitates and adds, "Each person deserves our respect, whether dead or alive. We perform these dissections and explorations to learn more about death so you can be caretakers of the living." Of course all of his words are in Italian.

He presses the blade into her chest; there is little blood, as much of it had already been drained from her body, but her skin splits open along the downward slice he makes toward her navel. I look at her pale face, eyes closed, lips together, no sign of pain. This is when my legs begin to express a slight wobble, hinting at a potential problem. The girl next to Marcello drops. He grabs her before she hits the floor. The guy at the woman's feet exits the room as I look his way. Neither one a useful distraction to my own vulnerability.

I feel like I'm on the table being cut...then I expect the woman to sit up reeling in pain, but she does not... there is little difference between me being alive and her being dead. She looks perfectly healthy, no obvious damage that could have caused death, but that little spark we call life is gone from her; it still lingers in me. An intangible weightless thing which keeps our hearts pumping, lungs expanding and contracting, and brains doing a million things to keep us alive. In my mind, I go back and forth between standing there and lying on the table beneath that blade. Benati cuts under and around each breast toward her armpits to form a "Y". Each slice seems to take a piece of me with it.

Benati cuts through several ribs to remove her heart. He holds it in both hands as if holding an injured bird, passes it to the student to his left, at the woman's head. The girl to my right hands it over to me. It is a hard muscle, heavy for its size, as big as a pair of praying hands with interlocking fingers. Facts from my college anatomy course flash through my mind. I'm holding an amazing life force that was beating a couple of days ago, over 100,000 times a day, forty million times a year. Had she lived to eighty it would have beat about three billion times.

I remember, as I hold it in my hands, it pumps blood through about 100,000 miles of blood vessels, enough to circle the Earth four times every minute. I look at it and think how often I have taken its diligent beating for granted? If it stops, any time we will die, and there is very little we can do to make sure it doesn't stop.

I struggle to resist imagining I'm on this table. I feel it's only luck I'm alive; the difference between life and death being indescribable, intangible, not measureable. I grip the cold marble table. I force myself to imagine she is a very accurate model of a human body, not someone who was actually alive just a day or two ago, talking, laughing, smiling, walking, eating, a mother, doing all the things living people do.

Then another organ of hers passes into my hands. It's half a football in size; one of her lungs. I'm in awe of our ability to breathe so effortlessly, without the slightest thought. A cold fact pops to mind. Lungs spread out flat would cover the area of a tennis court, but this doesn't explain their miraculous workings. I hold this soft grey lump of lung that oxygenated her body with about 23,000 inhales and exhales every day, eight million times a year. It now lies in my hands lifeless, of no value to anyone. I wonder, how many breaths I have left.

The crunching, snapping sound of each rib Benati cut to get to her heart and internal organs, with what looked like a very clean pair of small garden pruning shears, echoes in my mind the rest of the day and night. Seems it's that first time, even watching someone else do the cutting, that causes a kind of transference, between a living person and a dead human body, that poses the greatest chance of fainting.

Many years later I would find myself touching death again. This time it would be the moment that amazing spark of life leaves the body of someone I loved, and would be there no more.

■ ■ ■

A man goes into his doctor's office for an annual physical. After a while, the doctor comes out and says, "I'm sorry Bill, but you have a condition which only allows you another six weeks to live."

"But Doctor," Bill replies, "I feel great! I haven't felt better in years. This just can't be true. Isn't there anything I can do?"

After a moment the doctor says, "Well, you might start going down the street to that new health spa and take a mud bath every day."

Excitedly Bill asks, "And that will cure me?"

"No," replies the doctor, "but it will get you used to the dirt."

■ ■ ■

I was on a flight the other day when the air hostess came up to me and asks, "Excuse me sir, would you like to have dinner?"

I say, "What are the options?" She says, "Yes or No."

2

LIFE: OUR WORLD

I can describe life on our planet in four words: amazing, complicated, and incredibly diverse. I walked my dog the other day and counted over seventy-five different grasses, flowers, shrubs and trees, before returning home with the requisite bag of one of Harry's productions. Harry is my dog, and you know what dogs are best at producing.

There are about eight million different species of plants and animals on Earth, one-quarter of them in water and the remaining three-quarters on land. About 10,000 new ones are found each year. What an amazing planet. There are about 850,000 different insect species alone. All of this originally from single cells billions of years ago. Whoa!

During morning walks, from time to time, I've noticed a snail or two that had found its way through the wrought iron or picket fence spaces bordering gardens along the sidewalks that have been showered by sprinkler systems. During the few days there is actual rain in L.A., snails are out in much larger numbers. While making a slow steady trail across the pavement, from garden to garden, they potentially get into harm's way. It could be a texter's lack of attention resulting in a crushing death blow from a shoe, sneaker, or sometimes a mom's passing stroller wheel. In the worst case, it might be a person expressing their superiority to this little creature by purposely stomping on their fragile shell, extinguishing their life. Harry and I pick up these misguided mollusks, throw them over the fences they have navigated through, back into the shrubs and bushes, to potentially save their lives. Harry just watches, I do all the picking up and throwing.

Even as a kid I loved to read about biology. Whenever I found an insect in the house, whether the stinging kind or not, I captured it in a cup, then released it outside. I owe this to my Dad who did the same. As a kid, I never saw him stomp on any living thing. Yes, he slapped the occasional mosquito, as I have, to prevent a blood-sucking attack; self-defense. Today I am in awe of the complexity that goes into the smallest living things – the arrangement of tiny organs and parts that work perfectly together to allow them to walk, fly, reproduce, and be alive.

Have you ever seen the bad example provided by big brothers, sisters, friends, parents, or relatives who find it necessary to crush the life out of a tiny living creature? I bet this imprints a message and behavior that lasts with a child for their whole life. We should have a rule that if a person can make a tiny living creature, then, and only then, should they have permission to extinguish one of their lives.

Should this rule be in a chapter in the "How to be a Good Parent Handbook," given to every couple, or single person, who is about to become a parent, like the booklet we get to prepare each of us to be a new driver? Oh, yeah, there is no handbook or test required to become a parent... Do you think people who find pleasure in killing such lesser creatures tend to be more aggressive and less sensitive? Are these little creature-killers more apt to grow up and select reptiles for pets so they can feed them live food?

I'm amazed by the complexity of an insect like a fly, bee, or ant, and even more so by those really tiny ants or flying gnats? Their tiny hearts, blood vessels and breathing equipment all coordinate together so perfectly. We have in every cell of our bodies little power generator helping to keep us alive. Imagine if we needed sunlight, like plants for energy, we might only move around in the daytime and have to seek shelter every day by sunset. What a world that would be.

I see our lives exemplified in every flower. The bud possess unseen potential, blooming into something complex, fragile and beautiful, lasting a relatively short time, then withering and dying. It's worth greater because of its short existence, not unlike our own lives. When giving someone I care about, cut flowers about to bloom or in full bloom, I have always found truth in the saying, "Flowers whisper what words can never say."

When did you last stop for a moment to be in awe and appreciation of the complexity of our bodies? The oldest person just died at 122; recently, some scientists have come to believe human lifespan is about 115 years. There are others who think death is a disease, and if we treat it as such, we can find a "cure" or manage it better, like other diseases, extending healthy human lifespan to maybe 200 years. Presently we only live an average of about 32,000 days.

How about our eyes? We don't really "see" anything. Light bounces off objects in the world, passes through a lens then lands on nerve receptors in the back of our eyes. Electrical and chemical messages go to our brains which make up images we believe exist. Does every person's eyes work exactly the same? Does every one of our brains create the exact same images, shades, colors and textures? Or do we each "see" things just a little differently?

This gives me a little wiggle room in considering a tennis opponent's call that a tennis ball hits or misses the line. I believe most of the guys are not making a call just to win a difficult or important point. I'm confident, if attached to a lie-detector, they would be found to be truthful, because they believe their call is correct based on the way their brain created that image. No matter what the explanation, an out call results in a lost point. In baseball, in or out of the strike zone can affect the outcome of a game. But these are just games. The accuracy of our vision is so much more critical in many other life events.

I was surprised to find, as amazing as humans are, we only see, hear, and smell a fraction of the range of light, sounds, and scents present on planet Earth. A female moth, if it was the size of a human, may be able to attract a mate up to 50 miles away. Among closely related species, chemical sex attractants may only vary by a single atom, yet this difference is enough to be detected by animal sense organs far more sensitive than ours.

People are complex unique organisms, so to end one of their lives is incredibly horrible. The animal world still kills many humans each year. The greatest killers are mosquitos, killing about 850,000 people each year with the diseases they carry. Snakes are next, with 60,000 deaths, hippopotamuses account for about 500 deaths, elephants for a hundred, bees about sixty, Jellies around forty and sharks only six. And over 600,000 killings per year are at the hands of other people. Even in war, killing an enemy soldier, who is not directly threatening your life, is a tragedy of immense proportions. The death of innocent civilians, often called collateral damage, is horrific. It's no wonder abortion, euthanasia, and the death penalty are so hotly debated human issues.

We live on a fragile planet that fortunately is just far enough away from the sun to have liquid water and not too far or there would only be ice. Top priority for all governments is to protect our planet. If not for the scientific research that led to the Montreal Protocol twenty-five years ago, the ozone layer would have been destroyed by CFC from aerosol sprays and other sources, causing hundreds of millions of deaths from cancer, and agricultural disaster, leading to drastic food shortages across the planet. Science matters and politicians who do not do everything in their power to protect our fragile planet are an existential danger to humanity. Scientists tell us sea levels are likely to rise one to four feet by 2100 due to the planet warming if we don't stop heating the planet today. Many leaders with little to no scientific knowledge are ignoring this warning. This global warming causes ocean waters to expand and glaciers and polar ice caps to melt. This will impact at least five million people living in coastal communities just in the US. What are our leaders doing about climate change?

Yet, just how significant is the entire human race in our galaxy and universe? Sadly, rather insignificant. Astronomers tell us our sun is only one of billions of suns in our galaxy, which is only one of billions of galaxies in the universe, and many suns (stars) are bigger than ours. On a clear starry night, if you spin around, the band of stars you see across the sky is the side of our galaxy packed with the most density of stars. It has been described as a "milky way," which is how our galaxy got its name.

Next time you're at a beach, pick up a grain of sand. All the rest of the grains of sand on the beach, and likely more, represent less than the number of stars in the universe.

It has been estimated in our galaxy alone, there are over a million planets that could have all the right conditions for life like we find on Earth. Almost every one of them is much older than Earth; millions of years older. I believe, as do some other scientists, the chance of other intelligent life in just our galaxy, is almost certain, to say nothing about the chance of intelligent life elsewhere in the universe. Life on these planets are likely to be far more advanced than on our very young planet. Consider how much we have advanced in technology in just the past one hundred years. Can you imagine where the next 1,000 or 10,000 years will take us? What about 100,000 or a million years?

I have a blue grain of sand in a clear little box on my desk. I think of it as Earth. When I have a problem, I look at that sand grain and try to appreciate how insignificant my problems are in the scope of our galaxy, and even less important in our universe.

■ ■ ■

A frog goes to a fortune teller to find out if he will ever be lucky in love.

The fortune teller reads his webbed palm and tells the frog, "I have good news and I have bad news. Which would you like to hear first?"

The frog asks for the good news first.

The fortune teller says, "You are going to meet a pretty girl who is going to want to know all about you."

"Great," says the frog. "What's the bad news?"

"The bad news is you're going to meet her in biology class."

■ ■ ■

You are on a horse, galloping at a constant speed.

On your right side is a sharp drop-off, and on your left side is an elephant traveling at the same speed as you.

Directly in front of you is another galloping horse, but your horse is unable to overtake it.

Behind you is a lion running at the same speed as you and the horse in front of you.

What must you do to safely get out of this highly dangerous situation?...

Get your drunken ass off the merry-go-round!

3

FROM THE BEGINNING: PLEASURE

I believe humans are pleasure-seeking animals from our moment of birth. We seek the pleasure of human touch, a mother's breast and the comfort of just being held. Pleasure-seeking stays with us throughout our lives. Admiration is pleasure's aphrodisiac. We seek the adoration of others in one form or another whether in the adoration of our bodily looks, how we dress, our talents, wealth, who we know, and for some, our last performance. While admiration equals pleasure, I think depression is the absence of pleasure, and this is so powerful it might drive some to lose interest in the very essence of a continued life.

Pleasure accompanies every survival behavior, such as quenching thirst and eating. My friend Dick, an accomplished and creative retired network executive who brought the first Ice Capades to China, had been a heavy cigarette smoker. Several years before I met him, he switched to cigars to reduce his chances of lung cancer. Unfortunately, he contracted throat cancer and had to have part of his tongue removed.

Doctors initially assured him he would get off a liquid diet after three or four months, but they revised their prognosis, telling him his tongue would never be able to properly function again, other than for speech. Dick's tongue worked well enough for him to speak pretty clearly, which we all appreciated, since it served his terrific sense of humor. During Dick's difficulties, we learned the tongue is needed to move food from our mouths down our throats. Dick said he never realized how much pleasure there was in just simply eating. A couple of months after he mentioned this to us at the club, he stopped his feeding tube and liquid diet, starving himself to death.

Humans evolved from a common primate link between the Bonobos and Chimpanzees, six to seven million years ago. Over millions of years we evolved from walking on all fours to being bipedal primates on two legs, able to carry things as we roamed about. With this advantage came the disadvantage to males of having more difficulty easily and casually seeing female genitals, thus likely reducing frequent sexual activity. When I hear about some men showing their genitals to women, thinking it will be a turn-on to them, it strikes me as less a current phenomenon, but rather a bit of a throw-back to our more primitive male/female behaviors. While the site of a naked female body is a powerful stimulant to a male, it is likely less so for modern women.

Our DNA is still 98.6% to 99% the same as the Bonobos and Chimps. Modern humans, Homo sapiens, developed into a distinct species from the shared genetic pool of these two ancestors about 200,000 to 300,000 years ago.

It's understandable that we share many of their traits and behaviors, one of which is the use of tools to solve problems. Tattoo parlors and hair removal businesses are fortunate we have not maintained our ancestors' heavily hairy bodies. Chimpanzees have evolved in a male-dominated social order, with an omnivorous diet, consuming plants and animals, along with an aggressive nature. Bonobos bring to the genetic table a non-violent and cooperative behavior, influenced by their female-dominated social organization.

It's reported that over seven million years, primates have been promiscuous, having many sexual partners. Only in the past 10,000 years, since modern humans began to farm, did some form of monogamy take hold. This may be why our natural instinct to be with more than one partner is difficult to break, especially in light of the very short time monogamy has been practiced among primates during these past millions of years.

I can see how polygamy is so imprinted as a more human primal instinct than is monogamy, but social growth has seemed to favor the latter. Those who have made a business of such instinctual promiscuous behavior is what has victimized many women, not the process of sharing affections. It takes a disciplined male to completely tamp down these evolutionary urges for sexual variety once he has committed to a monogamous relationship. If this instinct was not so strong, there would be little market for pornography and prostitution.

This brings to mind a tennis friend who for ten years after his monogamous marriage ended, enjoyed the pleasure of dating a variety of women. He often spoke of how satisfying he found this lifestyle. Then one day on the courts he mentions he and the women he spent the most time with, who is in her forties, got married. Really! My first instinct was to feel sorry for him, to have given up what he described as his ideal sexual life. I asked, "What made you decide to give up variety for a single woman?" I expected a classic answer like, "I fell in love. She's all I want or need in my life." I didn't hear anything like this. Instead, he tells me, "We agreed I could still have sexual variety so long as I don't get involved emotionally or romantically with another women." Fair enough; sign me up and most other men I know! He went on to say, "Sometimes she brings home a girlfriend and the three of us have sex.". Where does fantasy end and reality begin? Now his choice to get married makes sense; a lot of sense. Could his relationship model be a harbinger of the future?

Kinsey and others found most males have a much stronger sex drive than most females at every stage of their lives. To an overwhelming number of men, a women's body is seen as a source of pleasure, so heterosexual men compete with other men for female attention. Thus we get the illusion that sex is the process of a woman being the giver and the man being the taker, rather than a mutual exchange of give and take. Is it possible that women over time are developing greater sex drives than in the past? If so, would we see women trying to get men to bed and competing rigorously with other women for men? Doesn't it appear to some degree already happening? From what I've read, surveys suggest women of younger generations are continuously seeking more sexual equality. It's a good thing, for so many reasons, for both men and women.

Tom and Sue: Married 20 years, very much in love - Tom gets paralyzed from the neck down, could last for 6 months or life. They both like and have sex a lot but now Tom can no longer do it.

Tom asks a good single friend if he would have safe, protected, non-romantic/emotional, sex with Sue now and then? Would his friend agree to help them if Sue is okay with it? Would he if he was married? Would his wife be okay with it?

Visa-Versa - Sue gets paralyzed knowing Tom's need for physical sex, would she ask a single girlfriend to have safe, non-romantic/emotional, protected sex with Tom now and then? Would her girlfriend agree to do this for Sue and Tom? What if she was married? Would her husband be okay with it?

No other person would know about this to avoid anyone else's judgement. **What would you do?** In the next five to ten years it would be two words; sex dolls.

What might the future hold? If I let my sci-fi imagination run a little wild, might we see gyms with a series of rooms where consenting couples, without exchanging payment, practice sexercise? One member invites another to meet them at their designated time, in a reserved room. Entering such a room, in a somewhat darkened hallway to maintain privacy and confidentiality, and then after the encounter exiting into either the men's or women's locker rooms. This would be the ultimate physical, safe, multiple partner, consensual exercise associated with extreme pleasure. In the sci-fi novel I wrote forty years ago , "Sorry, It's A Boy," There were sophisticated sex dolls and women chose double mastectomies to prevent breast cancer. The sexercise rooms are no more a radical concept than such surgeries, which for many women today is a real health option.

We don't have to look very far into the future to see a sex trend blossoming right now in the world. There are dozens of manufactures in the US and around the world making humanoid, life-sized (from 4 ½ feet to 6 feet tall) "sex dolls," weighing 50 to 80 pounds to meet the growing demand by men and women for sexual satisfaction without the baggage of dealing with another person. The production volume, in total, probably already exceeds 10,00 per month. They cost from about $500, to the most common ones priced at between $2,000 and $6,000. But for about $20,000 an Artificial Intelligence doll can have a conversation with their owner and initiate sexual activities.

When ordering a female sex doll, even at $500, the customer gets to select the face, skin, wig, genital hair (short, long or waxed smooth), eye color, and even nail polish color. The buyer also can choose height, physical dimensions of her breasts, waist, and hips, plus an assortment of outdoor clothing and night wear. They can also get one that maintains a human body temperature. Male dolls have substantial sized penises, and these dolls also come with clothing choices for a number of occasions. The male dolls are sold to serve both men and women users.

Why a "sex doll" vs a human companion? They beat masturbation which requires even more imagination. These are always available and for those that are not equipped with Artificial Intelligence, they will not argue, require a complicated relationship, and they will never cheat on their owners. Many young people can get frustrated trying to meet someone online or over a dating app. These dolls guarantee zero sexual frustration while waiting to find the right person for a sexual and emotional relationship. Recently a brothel has opened in Spain which provides only sex dolls to service customers. Life is complicated, will these make it simpler? They push the envelope and beg the question; does having sex with such a humanoid doll constitute cheating on your significant other, husband, or wife?

Evolution has fine-tuned us to find pleasure in every event and action that is healthy and extends our lives. Unfortunately many of us find pleasure in things that can shorten them as well. It's pleasurable detoxifying your body – emptying your bladder, eliminating feces, and even passing gas painlessly. We've all experienced discomfort or pain of one sort or another, so recognizing and appreciating when we feel just fine is a gift. It makes for a happier life. I'm certain it's no evolutionary accident that the process of increasing the species is the most pleasurable for all animals, humans included. Evolution has served us well, while those less served are now extinct.

A welcome touch can generate real benefits even on those who are fully clothed. A friend in graduate school did a study with her fellow waitresses. They touched half their male customers lightly on the shoulder, arm or hand, and found this resulted in higher tips. They also found such touching resulted in those customers drinking more alcohol.

I love the feeling of affectionate human touch. How many of us have found great pleasure by touching, caressing, and stimulating a partner to the point of their sexual satisfaction, even without it being mutual and simultaneous? While genital stimulation can bring about a satisfactory climax, I did not know an orgasm stimulates every major part of the brain. It may be less likely to happen without a ready and willing mind, making our grey matter, matter... clearly an essential sex organ.

On a lighter note, we've evolved with some simple but great physical features above and beyond all the pleasures. For instance, the length of our arms; what if they were much shorter? How would we wipe our asses? Evolution permitted dogs to lick their genitalia but not humans. Good thing! It might have resulted in many humans being pre-occupied and killed by predators and having less interest in heterosexual activities to promote our species. This is why physical features are best left to evolutionary design and not to people. The accommodating size of our nostrils and fingers – thicker fingers or smaller nostrils, or both, and nose-picking would never have evolved to the art we see today. Twigs would have been the tool of choice to evacuate ancient hair-lined nostrils, while more sophisticated, and probably jeweled, accessories might be used today to clear those nasal accumulations.

Hair is an important element of pleasure when touched or caressed, as is skin, our largest pleasure organ. From puberty, more and more hair appears on our bodies, continuing as we age. We can't get away from it; we're mammals first and foremost. Even elephants, whales, and porpoises have remnants of hair.

My dog, like most of our hairy or fur-covered pets, like to be petted. Each hair reaches below the skin, stimulating nerve endings. I don't know about you, but I love to have the hair on my head caressed or even moved around when I get a haircut. Not sure why it feels so good, maybe because it's so close to my brain.

Inevitably, hair will grow in inconvenient places. Removing it by waxing, an ancient technique, is still in big demand. Some hair is found in very personal, sensitive places, and during foreplay may be met by an affectionate tongue. This can be a bit off-putting during the passion of the moment. Most every adult has experienced this in the course of dating and lovemaking. It's no mystery where this hair appears… pesky ear hair. And while women rarely have ear hair to contend with, many wax away other body hair, making their mature bodies look and feel much younger and exciting to men. Again, natural instinct has driven male primates to younger females over millions of years because they were the ones most likely to bear children and continue the species.

With the help of modern medical advancements, women today have been able to fool "Mother Nature" by looking younger and more attractive with cosmetics and surgical enhancements. Thus many remain attractive to men for many more years than they would have thousands of years ago. Men have benefited just as much, if not more, with hair transplants and the same surgical magic, but they have sprung yet another trick on the natural order. While most senior men, in the distant past, would have been unable to even have intercourse, no less produce viable sperm for a desirous younger woman, pharmaceuticals can now extend that ability for men nearly to the doorsteps of death.

I was personally disadvantaged in college, having attended before the popularity of Brazilian waxing. I lived in a private house off campus in my junior year with four other guys. We all became good friends, so much so that while none of us joined college fraternities we formed our own. We called it Tappa Kegga Day (TKDelta). Our sweatshirts were maroon with white letters. As TKDelta, we rented the American Legion hall in town once a month, on a Sunday night. The whole college was invited – five dollars for guys and one dollar for girls, for all the beer they could drink until midnight. We made enough money each month to buy some groceries for our house.

During those college days we acted like our primate relatives, not only seeking promiscuous pleasure, but easily finding willing partners. It was the sixties. The downside, before HIV screwed things up, and when STDs were all treatable, were "crabs." These little clear crab-like creatures could spread through a college campus like a breeze on a spring day. One day I had the horrible surprise to find I too had come under attack and infestation. Because of our sexual freedom, I had no idea who had generously shared this gift with me, nor did I have any idea how to rid myself of them. It would have been bad form to go around asking even the most likely suspects if they too had become host to these little mischievous creatures.

University campuses would have been less crabby if women were into Brazilian waxing, but no such luck; it wasn't in vogue. I generally turned to the elder in our house, Bob, for advice of all kinds. Bob and Don worked for IBM in Fishkill, New York, across the Hudson River from our college. They stayed at the house Monday to Friday to attend graduate classes at night, going home to wives and kids on weekends. Bob claimed to have had personal combat experience with these nasty little critters so I thought I had come to the right guy. It was after dinner, all the guys in house were there to give me moral support and glean some knowledge from Bob.

His first words of wisdom were very reassuring. "Steve, no problem. It's easy to get rid of them and you can share this simple treatment with the girl who shared this gift with you. In fact, it only takes a few minutes and I can walk you through the easy steps." Great, I was all ears.

"Hey, Bob, I don't know who gave them to me, so it'll just be me following your plan." Quickly getting rid of this social scourge would reduce my abstention from dating.

He continued, "First, you get naked, but make sure the lights are very dim so you don't scare them into burrowing deeper into your pubic hair."

Made sense, Bob thought of everything – they seemed to like the darkness behind my jockey shorts. "Then you shave one half of your pubic area."

Okay, delicate but possible. Certainly easier for girls without the lumps and bulges in that area that make up my anatomy.

Bob went on, "Sit down and relax for at least fifteen minutes so any crabs still on the shaved side have time to scamper across to the hairy side. Remember keep those lights dimmed during this phase as well." A bit bizarre but I'd do most anything, a dip in ice water, stand on my head, anything to rid myself of these things.

"Okay, now you're ready for the final step. Now this is the most important part… set fire to the hairy side and when the "crabs" run across the shaven area, hit them with a hammer."

Bob had the most contagious laugh. He could hardly help from falling off his chair while the other guys couldn't contain their hysteria. After a good belly laugh he said, "No, seriously, just go to the infirmary and they'll give you a cream. It'll get rid of them in a week." His second suggestion worked just fine, but sexual dating had to be suspended.

Danny, one of my housemates, had an idea for part of our summer vacation that year. He figured his friend Joe could join us in a trip to Arizona and find the "Lost Dutchman's Gold Mine" in the Superstition Mountains. Dozens of fortune hunters had searched for it since it was discovered by the Spaniards over a century ago. Based on Danny's research, The Superstition Mountains were thought to be cursed by the Apache Thunder God. Reportedly, dozens of men were brutally massacred, died mysterious deaths, were led to insanity or disillusion, or just disappeared into thin air. What more could one ask for during a two-week summer vacation from college? So the three of us did a bit more research about this legendary huge gold mine before our trip.

Joe flew into Arizona from Colorado, where he was living at the time, and Danny and I came in from New York. After landing in Arizona we made our way to Globe, Arizona, the typical staging area from which most expeditions began before entering the Superstitions. The Peralta family from Sonora, Mexico, discovered the mine around 1845. They arranged to haul tons of gold back to Mexico by mules a year later. It's said the Apaches attacked them, killing 148 men, only two escaped the massacre. Many stories and maps appeared over time, but no one had yet found this incredibly wealthy gold mine. But here comes Danny, Joe, and Steve.

We go to a local stable in Globe that offers horseback riding along the local trails. We want to rent three horses to go into the Superstition Mountains for several days. The guy we speak to probably wants to say, "Are you joking?" His expression certainly says that after he looks us up and down; three Long Island eastern dudes. He puts his foot up on a rail, "Well guys, if I rent them horses to ya, I'd be takin their full price as a deposit, cauz I won't be specting them back alive."

Of course we ask, "Why is that? He replies, "Ya know they need water and food, every day. How'd ya plan for that?" The short answer is, we didn't. Something that was left out of all the westerns we watched as kids. He had us for sure, so we dropped the horse-renting plan.

We decide to go in by foot. He is happy to mention the goodly number of people found dead or just plain missing after leaving Globe and heading into the mountains. And adds, "If a rattler don't kill ya, some crazy guys in them mountains will kill ya, just for the clothing on ya back." Very reassuring. He must have been in charge of Globe's tourist bureau.

Okay, Plan B; we visit a gun shop and buy three handguns, holsters, and ammunition. There was no such thing as a background check then. Cash bought whatever you wanted. We'd have to protect ourselves from whatever might come at us, including "them crazy guys."

We each take a canteen of water, bed rolls, some food and other gear and off we march into the mountains heading for Weaver's Needle, a landmark identified in the most authentic maps discovered. After a couple of hours of walking we find a place to sit and rest under a mesquite tree. It's hot as hell and this tree only has tiny little leaves. We practice drawing our guns and shooting at targets we set up on the rocks nearby.

We find an abandoned mine opening on the side of a hill, but it's blocked off with rocks, maybe from a cave-in, but we never get further than a few feet inside.

We never saw a single person or rattlesnake all the time we spent in the mountains. We saw a rabbit and a few lizards. It was good to spend time with friends knowing we depended on each other for our safety. I have never been in the army or to war, but I imagined how much more intense it is for our soldiers when they are actually under fire from people trying to kill them, and having to depend on fellow soldiers for their lives. We all gained a far greater respect for our men and women in combat than we could ever have had by hearing the news reports of our soldiers in Vietnam.

I got to visit Vietnam, both Ho Chi Minh City (Saigon) and Hanoi a few years ago, many years after I was invited to go by our military during the sixties. I found the people so friendly and the country busy building in every direction. It made me feel even sadder that so many people had been killed, on both sides, seemingly for nothing. Like many recent wars, there are no winners, just those who lose their lives or loved ones.

■ ■ ■

While away from home in college a student writes a letter to his dad.

It says: "No mun, no fun, your loving son."

His father writes back saying: "Too bad, so sad, your loving dad."

■ ■ ■

The sergeant-major growls at a young soldier, "I didn't see you at camouflage training this morning."

The soldier replies, "Thank you very much, sir."

4

FAMILY: A WORLD OF HIGHS AND LOWS

Physical excitation is not the only powerful force that can provide deep-seated satisfaction and pleasure. I've found relatives, children, and friends, can also provide real pleasures that can fill a person with a sense of worth, pride, and fulfillment. Not the momentary exhilarating kind, but feelings that can last longer and become imbedded in our memories forever. I'm convinced life is a different experience for those people who have children. Not necessarily better, but definitely different. A recent study suggests having children can increase human life expectancy by about two years. This is probably not 100% true, because some people complain their child or children are "killing" them!

I wanted to be a father; maybe it was due to growing up in a family of four boys. It was not about passing on my name or genetics to the next generation. It's been about expanding my own life experiences. I remember when I found that my wife was pregnant I told her, "You be the primary parent until the kid can reason, then I'll get more involved." Well that didn't last. I was connected to that little guy the moment we had him home. I knew we were responsible for helping him have a happy, healthy, and meaningful life. It's an awesome responsibility, definitely life-changing. I was going to be the best parent ever, like I think every parent starts out to be but it is a struggle to avoid some of the less than perfect behaviors we've learned from our own childhoods. The one thing I tried was to not only criticize my son when he did something wrong, to help him do it better and right the next time, but to also praise him when he did something right. I got it right a lot, but sometimes, probably too often fell back to correcting him.

There are many more opportunities for a person to expand their interests, needs, and desires when caring about a child's life as they grow and interact with the world around them. To some degree I vicariously live through my son's life, the ups and downs, particularly when he does something good, something I could never have done. For a parent, when their child becomes a renowned artist or musician, a great teacher, an accomplished scientist, or even a terrific mother or father, there is a huge amount of pride.

■ ■ ■

Our son Josh was an average high school student with no sports or major accomplishments that would make him stand out among other highly qualified candidates. Like me, he was an average student, actually better than me. After visiting the GW campus in D.C., he decided it was the school he wanted to attend. Almost immediately I could imagine his pain and devastation if he didn't get accepted. Why do people so often go to the worst scenario? The barrier for acceptance would be great. His SAT scores were average, and acceptance to this school was a real challenge, even for the best students from around the country.

On his application he requested an interview. He was a good writer and a "people person." Several weeks later they notified him of his scheduled interview during his on-campus visit. We guarded our anxiety over him getting accepted, since many students who applied to this school were valedictorians, salutatorians, yearbook editors, class officers or outstanding athletes with exceedingly high SAT scores. We never expressed our reservations or discouraged him. The day of his interview my wife and I walked around the school's campus. Over lunch, our anxious thoughts focused on how he was doing at his interview. When we met him after-wards, we were eager to hear exactly how it went. Over dessert, chocolate ice cream for him and my wife, and a slice of apple pie for me (I love apple pie), he laid it all out.

He sits at a table across from a man and a woman who are on the admissions committee. They have a set number of items on their interview agenda to cover and discuss, then offer to answer all his questions about GW. At the end of the interview he asks if they would stay another minute or two so he can show them a card trick. Josh tells them he has an interest in magic and attended the internationally renowned "Tanner's Magic Camp" on Long Island for two summers. Tanner's was staffed by great magicians from around the country, with international guest magicians scheduled every week. The interviewers agree to stay and they sit back down.

Josh takes out a deck of cards. It must be a requirement for magic practitioners to always carry one. He pulls three cards from the deck and shows them to the two interviewers. There is an Ace of Hearts on one end, a Six of Clubs in the middle, and a King of Diamonds on the other end. He places the three cards, face down, in front of them, and asks one of them to slide out the middle card, keeping it face down against the table. The women interviewer slides the middle card out. Josh lifts the other two cards, shows them the Ace of Hearts and the King of Diamonds, places them back into the deck. Before they get to turn over the face-down card, he asks, "Do you remember the card under your fingers?" They look at each other for a moment, then both say, "The Six of Clubs." The woman turns over the card. It's not the Six of Clubs. It's a blank card with the fol-lowing printed on its face; **"I look forward to the magic of attending George Washington University."**

It was a very long three weeks before the letter from GW arrived. We were tempted to open it before Josh got home from school, but resisted. Before dinner, we sat around the kitchen table as he opened his letter... He was accepted! I insisted he had to break the magician's code, just this once, to show me how that trick was done.

Six years later, while studying for his Masters and Doctorate at GW, Josh worked for the university supervising housing units as a part-time job. He was curious, so he went to the admissions office and looked up his admissions folder. In the folder was that card with the statement he had written stapled to his application. The admissions people had placed a note on his application, which read, *"Recommended for acceptance based on his potential."* An amazing turning point in his life, all due to his own efforts.

Since graduation from GW he has built a career as a university administrator, taking on better jobs at each move. After working at GW he went on to Dartmouth, then NYU, to Bucknell, then an Associate Dean at Whittier College in California and now at Tufts University in Boston. We could not have experienced and shared his joy, or been impressed by his creativity, had we not had him as our child. There are many proud parents of terrific kids who have grown up to become good people. Parents, to some degree, live through their children's lives. These children can be the people who care about us as much as our parents have, assuming we've had a good relationship with our parents and kids.

■ ■ ■

I know things don't always go so well, and many parents must struggle with their children as they become adults. Good parenting is not easy and should never be underestimated. My wife says, "Parents get what they raise." I'm sure there's also an element of luck, and we have been very lucky. Sometimes genetics and social interactions create personalities and shocking behaviors over which parents have little control or ability to provide significant guidance. There are two sides to that "having children" coin. While they can bring incredible joy, they can also bring anguish and conflict into your life, like no other person can, because their pain will be your pain.

A friend of ours has a daughter currently serving a life sentence in a Texas State Prison, convicted of murder. She was hanging out with two guys she knew, when she overheard them discussing a robbery. She didn't participate in any other way. But under Texas law, since the robbery ended in a murder, she was deemed as guilty as the men who committed the robbery and shot the victim, just for having known about it in advance.

Shortly after moving to L.A., about thirteen years ago, I met Abee at the tennis club. He introduced me to many of the members I still play tennis with each week. When my son came to visit us in California for the first time, Abee and his wife, both psychologists, invited us to their home for dinner. Josh was about twenty-three and they had a daughter who was about nineteen. This was not a dating set-up; it was just so everyone would have someone with common interests to talk with over dinner. They lived in Abee's childhood home where they raised their daughter after his parents died. It was tucked into a tree-lined country-like side road, off a main canyon road.

The sun was shining that winter day, and as New York transplants we loved the humidity-free, seventy-eight degree weather. Sweet-smelling flowers and lush green trees abounded along the picturesque drive to their home. Of course there were many palm trees, for what would L.A. be without them? Flowers and palm trees make great backdrops in photos sent back to New York friends digging out from frozen weather and snowstorms. It was so friendly and neighborly of Abee and his wife to invite us for our first visit to a California home. What a lovely family.

Abee's house is built on the side of a hill. The driveway points skyward. After driving in, coming to a stop, I stand on the emergency brake pedal while blood rushes to my brain. Gravity tries to keep us from opening the doors, but we manage to escape the car. We climb the steps to the front door, Abee meets us with his broad engaging smile. I hand him a bottle of Cabernet. We enter their home. His wife is to our right in the kitchen. The kitchen/dining room table is ahead of us. The whole area to our left opens to the living room.

His wife moves around the kitchen like an expert chef. She turns to us with a big smile, "Welcome to California!" She comes over and gives my wife and me a hug. "Dinner will be ready in about fifteen minutes." She tells Abee, "Don't just hold the bottle, open it for our guests, have a seat and a drink while I finish up here." She calls out to her daughter who is in another room. Their daughter walks into the living room as Abee pours the wine.

She was "model beautiful." Just what one would expect of the stereo-typical California girl – long blonde hair, tan body, terrific figure, smartly dressed, with a radiant, warm, welcoming smile. I thought to myself, this was a beautiful family. Abee wasn't that beautiful, but seemed like a good guy.

She and my son talk a little about their schools and who knows what else, while we chat with Abee about tennis, the club, restaurants he recommends in the area, and other things we should do now that we're living in California. In what seems like a minute or two, his wife calls over to her daughter, "Honey, would you finishing setting the table, we're just about ready to sit down." Her daughter, without hesitation, finishes setting the table; what a good kid. She's like an angel. Her mother presents a fresh salad as we all take seats at the large table. My wife, Josh, and I sit on one side and their family is on the other side. A large bowl of fresh cut fruit, berries, and a pie sit on a side counter for dessert. Whoa! California is turning out to be such a great place – wonderful weather, healthy foods, and good people.

Halfway through the main course, a choice of chicken or tuna steak, and fresh-cooked vegetables, their daughter says, "Dad, I'm going over to friends' tonight, need to borrow your car." Abee has a sporty red convertible, his wife has a new-model sedan. "Sure, but I need it for tennis early tomorrow morning." His daughter takes a couple bites of food, replies, "I'm going to stay overnight and won't be back 'til later tomorrow." Abee is nonchalant, "Okay then, take Mom's car." His daughter looks over, past her Mom, at Abee. "No..." She takes a drink of her wine. "My friends think your car is mine. I need to use it." Abee calmly responds between a bite of food and a sip of wine, "Okay then, just get it back sometime tonight."

Apparently an unseen fuse had just been lit.

His daughter jumps up, slams her fork down, looks directly at Abee and shouts, "You fucking selfish bastard...you piece of shit..." Her mother interrupts, "Stop your damn yelling." Her daughter glares at her, eyes ablaze, "Stop taking his side. Fuck you too!" She dumps her plate into the sink with a crash. "I'm taking the fucking car, I don't give a damn what you say." She heads for the front door. All our heads turn toward the door. Abee leaps to his feet, gets to the door before her. "You little bitch, I'm putting the lock on my steering wheel, there's no way in hell you're taking my car!" She turns away, marches to a room off the kitchen, turns as she opens the door. "Fuck you both, I hate you." Our heads snap in her direction. Abee yells back, "Fuck you too." We look back toward Abee. She slams the door behind her as Abee rushes out the front door to his car.

The three of us, on our side of the table were stunned, mouths agape, eyes bulging in shock. "Hello…we are sitting right here," could have been my reasonable comment at that moment. Then a thought flashed through my mind. I felt an instinct to stand and applaud. After all, this was L.A., land of movies, actors and Hollywood. Was this a great performance or what? I expected them both to re-enter from stage doors left and stage door right to take their bows for an amazingly talented performance. This might have been quite an exciting theatrical addition to a great dinner. But it wasn't.

His wife busies herself cleaning off a few dishes when Abee stomps through the front door, a bit out of breath from the climb back up the stairs from the garage. He does not enter for a bow, instead announces to his wife, "I'm going to lie down." He goes past us, without a word, to his bedroom and closes the door. His daughter does not make an entrance for her bow either. His wife waits for him to disappear into their bedroom, turns to us and says, "He's out for the night, would you like some dessert?"

As I meet more families I'm convinced the joys of parenting can take us to amazing and enjoyable heights, or to the depths of despair. This reinforces my thought that there should be a test to become a parent, and if not, at least a short required course. Even pass/fail could be helpful. The big question is; are people who have kids more or less happy than those who choose not to have kids. We may never know for sure.

∎ ∎ ∎

A little girl asks her father, "How did the human race appear?"

The father answers, "God made Adam and Eve; they had children; and so was all mankind made."

Two days later the girl asks her mother the same question.

The mother answers, "Many years ago there were monkeys from which the human race evolved."

The confused girl returns to her father and says, "Dad, how is it possible you tell me the human race was created by God, and Mom says we developed from monkeys?"

The father answers, "Well, Dear, it is very simple. I told you about my side of the family, and your mother told you about hers."

■ ■ ■

A wife gets so mad at her husband she packs his bags and tells him to get out.

As he walks to the door she yells, "I hope you die a long, slow, painful death."

He turns around and says, "So, you want me to stay?"

5

SELF-REFLECTION: WHAT'S TO LIKE – NOT TO LIKE

I don't know if any autobiographical book is complete, or even entirely honest, if the author doesn't reflect upon his or her own shortcomings, and take responsibility for them. We all have flaws and are not perfect. I see this imperfection as an affirmation of our humanity. It therefore should not be a surprise why not everyone we meet likes us. The flip side of this is why can't we like everyone we meet? Being in harmony with all those around us is often difficult. Is it that personality traits we see and dislike in others are part of our own behaviors?

I bristle when I heard someone say, "Just ask Steve, he knows everything." I know this is patently false, but why would someone say this? I'm an avid reader, having spent many years in college getting advanced degrees, so I've learned a little about a lot of things, and a tremendous amount about some things. Was it my behavior that gave that person such an opinion? Or does someone say this just to be aggravating? To take control of this possible perception I must address the former question. Firstly, I'm very opinionated and this may come off as arrogant, or a "know it all." Since perception is reality, I must take any such perceptions seriously. I now make a conscious effort to blunt statements of certainty by beginning many of my comments with, "In my opinion..." Also I found I can convey my thoughts in the form of a question and not seem to come off as an authority.

Secondly, having been raised in the Bronx, saying things with certainty is a New York City, Bronx dialect. This is also true for the use of off-color language from time to time, which may offend some people. I'm trying to curb this, but it's easier said than done. I have started by not making comments on the tennis courts, probably my place with the most flashpoints for such utterances. I've heard someone say, "Vulgarity is the inability of the feeble-minded to express themselves forcefully." I have no idea who said this, but I'm sure it's not entirely true, but it does seem that using a vulgar word to strongly express a feeling is a lazy use of language.

When people in a group discussion frequently brings the subject back to themselves, I find it irritating. Thus I look at my own behavior to determine if this is something I unconsciously do from time to time when I'm in a conversation with others. It's very hard not to do this since most of us innately believe our lives are the most important and interesting. I'm committed to minimizing such behavior if it resides in my pattern of conversational interactions. I've become a better observer of things I find objectionable in others, which prompts me to be introspective, ridding or reducing myself of such similar behaviors.

Thoughts about being liked or disliked by others brings to mind the injustice of racists, anti-Semites and xenophobes, because these people who hold such prejudices are not reacting to an individual's personal behavior, but to intrinsic characteristics that cannot be changed. Therefore, leaving no way to make the interactions with such people better.

■ ■ ■

Some questions, thoughts, likes and dislikes, that come to mind.

- A hug is a powerful expression of affection because our beating hearts are inches apart, something that rarely happens except between lovers.
- I have recently been trying to live according to 14th-century Zazen Yojinki: Eight parts of a full stomach sustain the man; the other two sustain the doctor.

- I like people who smile.
- In about 100 years everyone over the age of 10 will be dead. Many will have helped others while some will have done harm; is it so hard to choose to be one or the other?
- If today was Saturday or Sunday, seems many people will call the week that follows, this week, while others will call it next week; seems confusing.
- Ancient human bodies lying together naked was for warmth. Today it's an affectionate expression of sexuality blocked by even a single layer of clothing.
- I like people who pick up after their dogs and don't leave their dog's "dump" for others to find beneath their shoes or sneakers.
- In my senior years I find the more joy and pleasure I have in each day, the longer my life seems?
- I don't like people who drop their cigarette butts on walkways, treating them like paths through the middle of a giant ashtray.
- If time travel is ever possible, why hasn't anyone from the future come to visit?
- I like people who are not late for meetings and get-togethers; it's respectful of the time of the other people who they are meeting.
- Like heat-seeking missiles, people are pleasure seeking animals.
- When I'm sleeping in the fetal position, I wonder if my hands, arms, and feet are in the exact same positions as they were when I was in the womb?
- I like people who keep their word, rather than those who make unfulfilled promises.
- If you hold in farts before getting on a scale, does the gas give you just a little lift, so you weigh just a little less?
- I don't like it when people spit on the street.
- I like people who take their trash out of a theatre and don't leave it for someone else to pick up; it's just good manners.
- The longer a couple is together, the more I think they become friends with common interests and less of energetic sex partners.

- Primitive humans did not drink the milk of other animals, so why after getting off our mothers' milk do many humans? This doesn't seem to be healthy.
- I like people who hold the door open for someone right behind them.
- I don't like to hear people say "my bad"; it's so "following the crowd," and a lazy way of saying, "sorry, my mistake."
- In the great paintings of the renaissance, Adam and Eve have navels? Based on religious teachings, wouldn't this be wrong?
- I like to see dads with their kids.
- I don't like people who get phony "Service Dog" attire to bring their pets with them to cheat the system.
- I like friends who ask, "How you doing?" when they know you're having some health or life issues.
- Recognizing mortality awakens most of us to the importance of everyday living.
- I'm disappointed by the so many, who have so much, giving nothing, not even their consideration and respect to those who have so little.
- I don't like it when women wear so much perfume they travel in a cloud, leaving a tell-tale trail behind them.
- I like people who put out bird feeders, or just feed the birds.
- I never worry. If worrying helped, there would be courses in college on how to worry.
- I don't like people who use handicap parking tags that are not theirs, or they no longer need.
- I like drivers who let you in front of them when you use your directional, rather than speeding up to prevent you from changing lanes.
- Why don't I ever see birds die while flying, then drop from the sky to the ground?
- I like the way the Vietnamese women at a manicure shop speak so softly and still carry on a conversation across the room.
- I don't like to see predatory people make believe they are homeless and needy, begging on the streets, to prey on the good will of people who hand them money.

- I like people who adopt rescue dogs and cats.
- I don't like noisy restaurants requiring voices to be raised to be heard across a table.
- I respect those people who appreciate how difficult it is to turn 100 blank pages into a good screenplay or 150 to 300 pages into a book.
- Whenever I ask for a referral, everyone says they have the best doctor, best dentist, best accountant or best lawyer in town. Really?
- I don't like it when people use phony excuses to get out of jury duty; not only is it an obligation of citizenship, but a privilege not provided in every country.
- I like people on the tennis courts or walkways who DO NOT step on insects, just because they can.
- I don't like it when people leave the lights on when they're not in the room.
- I like people who adopt children.
- Primitive humans did not just go out for a jog, and they definitely never ran on pavement, so how could this possibly be any good for the human body?
- I don't like it when people waste water by leaving it run more than necessary.
- I love meeting and spending time with strangers; some of them will become my friends for the rest of my life.
- I liked hearing my son laugh when he was a baby and young kid, and I still like hearing him laugh as an adult.
- I don't like men slamming a second serve return at a woman by the net to win a point; it's just a game, not worth hurting anyone.
- I like people at buffets who eat all they take.
- There is so much pleasure in just living; little things like emptying our bladder or a good bowel movement, without discomfort, feels so good. The young should enjoy it while they can.
- I don't like people behaving entitled, cutting across double lines into an HOV lane, possibly putting others in harm's way to get injured or killed.

- It's not true that "Knowledge is power." Rather "Applied Knowledge is Power." Knowing a stove top is hot is not power, not touching a hot stove top is power.
- I like people who return a "Hello" as you pass them on the street.
- I wonder what our dogs and cats are thinking when their staring eyes feel like they're piercing our hearts.
- I don't like people who get pleasure hurting others, even if only by words.
- A friend is someone who says nice things about you behind your back.
- It's saddens me that the bad, foolish, hurtful, evil, and thoughtless behavior we hear in the news or see in life makes me believe the best explanation is to start with the premise; most, many or the average human being is a moron.
- And finally, as much as we try there is no way to avoid making mistakes as long as we live, so my only hope is they get smaller and less painful.

■ ■ ■

A guy spots a sign outside a house that reads "Talking Dog for Sale." Intrigued, he walks in.

"So what have you done with your life?" he asks the dog.

"I've led a very full life," says the dog. "I lived in the Alps rescuing avalanche victims. Then I served my country in Iraq. And now I spend my days reading to the residents at a retirement home."

The guy is flabbergasted. He asks the dog's owner, "Why on earth would you want to get rid of an incredible dog like that?"

The owner says, "Because he's a liar! He never did any of that!"

■ ■ ■

A guy notices an attractive woman in the supermarket waving at him. As he gets closer she says, "Hello."

He's rather taken aback because he can't place where he knows her from. "Do you know me?"

To which she replies, "I think you're the father of one of my kids."

Now his mind travels back to the only time he has ever been unfaithful to his wife and says, "My God, are you the stripper from my bachelor party I made love to on the pool table with all my buddies watching?"

She looks into his eyes and says calmly, "No, I'm your son's teacher."

6

SEXUALITY: WOMEN ARE SUPERIOR TO MEN

I am writing this book from my perspective as a straight male. I've come to believe sexual preferences are not learned, nor is it a choice. Seems we are born with an attraction to one sex or the other, and no amount of education and training will reverse this biological inclination. Promoting it as a choice seems to be a cruel untruth fostered by some who have been indoctrinated by organized religions. If gayness was learned by humans there would be no gayness in the natural world. This same natural world created by the God followers of many organized religions worship, and who they suggest created all life on Earth. Yes, this same God they also claim frowns upon such non-heterosexual behavior. But what is the reality...the truth? How do their "God's creatures" actually behave?

A little research indicates 8-10% of rams prefer male partners as do about 25% of male black swans. Not to be outdone by the males of the world, 10-15% of female seagulls prefer other female seagulls. These sexual preferences have also been noted by biologists among elephants and giraffes. And while these animals are very distant from our species, homosexual behavior has also been observed among all primate species including the great apes, and our closest evolutionary relatives, Bonobos and Chimpanzees.

The anatomical differences between males and females are apparent to all of us. A man has one opening, through his penis to both eliminate waste (urine) and deliver sperm for reproduction. This delivery mechanism, during aging, becomes less able to perform sexual intercourse, making older males of the tribe less attractive to young capable childbearing women. At least that was the way it was before the pharmaceutical companies found a drug to extend the life of an erect penis. When it comes to facts about erect penises I was surprised to find a British international study in March of 2015 of 15,000 men, that found the average length of an erect penis, which has no link to race, is 5.2 inches. It enlarges from the average flaccid penis size of about three and one half inches. A man's brain, in many instances, will have an exaggerated perception of size, but whether grounded in reality or not, a man's brain will still drive him to having sex for as long as possible, into very old age.

Women are anatomically superior having a vagina for reproduction, and a separate opening to eliminating waste (urine) through the urethra. I was surprised to learn a woman's vagina is only three to four inches long, but with the ability to expand to almost double its size when excited. This is a greater percentage increase than a flaccid penis can grow to full erection. As a woman ages she does not need a drug to extend her sexual organ's ability to have intercourse, except for the possible need for a lubricant. She can continue an active sex life for as long as she lives. It's the woman's brain that belies her continued interest in sex, at or near the same level of a man's, as she ages.

The genesis of powerful males, taking advantage of females, began millions of years ago. It continued in ancient civilizations thousands of years ago. The most powerful men among primitive humans and ancient civilizations were able to take the women they wanted. Many women sought the attention of such men in the tribe who could protect and provide for them and a family. While it's been wired into our evolutionary instincts, there is no excuse to shackle such abhorrent behavior today in modern societies, where women and men are recognized as equals.

Primitive humans and primate ancestors were promiscuous, and this promiscuity involved both male and female partners. In recent studies of Bonobos, it was found sex was used as appeasement, affection, stress reduction, and even for erotic games. Early humans could see other animals having sex and would have been fascinated by human birth, but I can't imagine they related intercourse with childbirth. Sexual pleasure was always a good thing, otherwise I might not be writing this and you might not be reading it. Sex had to then, as now, be fun. Organized religions clamped down hard on women regarding chastity and monogamy. It's understandable since these religions were written, taught, and managed by men. This behavior favored the men in relationships.

■ ■ ■

But this book is about people today and my journey in life. My sexual preference is for women, although if I had been born with an interest in other males, I expect I would be as passionate about them as I am passionate about women. Each of us discovers sexuality during our unique paths to adulthood. I am sure I'm not alone in recognizing sexuality as a central theme and source of great pleasure and joy in our lives, whichever our preferences.

At the ripe old age of eleven or twelve, I was growing up in the "Projects" on Harrod Avenue in the Bronx. I lived in apartment 3H, at the end of a long hall, in one of those high-rise buildings filled with minority families – Hispanics, Blacks, Jews and Catholics. Even then I was attracted to girls. They were distinguished by long hair, the tone of their voices, dresses, and softer mannerisms. I remember two in particular, Georgina and Carolyn. I liked Carolyn who had long straight flowing hair, while Georgina had shorter curly hair. They were always together, wore skirted Catholic school uniforms, and didn't attend P.S. 48, which was the elementary school I walked to each day. They had shapeless bodies then, indistinguishable from the boys.

Our winters were full of football games and sledding, while spring and summer were occupied by bicycling to the Bronx Zoo, roller skating, and stickball. We played in the street with one car on each side of the road designated as first and third bases; second base and home plate were chalked in the middle of the road. The girls in the neighborhood did their girl things, we guys did our guy things, never together. But on occasion the girls would watch our stickball game.

Our team was called the Red Devils and our uniforms were simply a Red Devil patch sewn on our tee-shirts by our mothers. I remember four of my closest friends on the team – Sonny was a tall black kid; Victor was Hispanic; Howard was Jewish; and Shawn was Catholic. Some things you just never forget. I also remember how good it felt to get a great hit or make a terrific catch when the girls were watching. Even then, admiring looks from the females of our species added a great deal of pleasure to a good performance. Most boys liked the adoration of girls and I've seen it continue through high school, college and to some degree into adulthood. But it seems to me, due to the media, adoration of men by girls and women has mostly changed from being impressed by personal performances to the possession of fancy cars, homes, expensive jewelry, and all kinds of things. How much simpler it must have been when all we had was our naked good-looking selves to offer a possible mate.

■ ■ ■

I am a late starter when it comes to sex. In my sophomore year of college, Jan, my friend Hank's girlfriend introduces me to Elaine on a blind date. She does not have a cheerleader's body, she is more filled out than that, but still attractive with a playful personality. On our second or third date, following a movie, we return with Hank and Jan to the house Hank is renting. After a couple of joints and some wine, Jan and Hank retire for the night and tell us to just close the front door when we leave. We both are feeling very relaxed and affectionate. Whoa! "What a perfect opportunity for having sex." This is what goes through my horny college mind.

I have never had real sex, other than the occasional kiss and caressing clothing covering a girl's breast. But now I'm with a girl who seems receptive to being a lover. We go into the guest room, illuminated just enough by the street lamp flickering through the swaying branches of a tree outside the window. Her body clothed does not seem all that attractive, but when we undress, and are naked, I see her as a magnificent goddess.

Touching, kissing, our hands and bodies intertwine in every which way. It is exhilarating. My level of excitement rises with each fondling touch of her warm breasts and soft body. After a few minutes, she and I are ready to maneuver ourselves into position for the ultimate pleasure of the night. BAM… I climax… resulting in a gooey mess all over the both of us. This performance is a disaster, like striking out at stickball with all the girls watching. I don't want her to know this is my first time, but she probably figures it out. How embarrassing. She is clearly more experienced than me.

Elaine was incredibly comforting, telling me it was probably too much wine. The following weekend, I was sure not to have any wine. We had sex and it was the most pleasurable and exciting thing I had ever done. I knew right then and there that the best place on planet Earth is in a consenting woman's vagina. I believe most every heterosexual man carries this feeling and belief with him his entire life. Yes, Paris is romantic, London historic and Tahiti is beautiful, but none of these compare to this intense pleasure. It's a driving force within us men that continues into adulthood and beyond. I have made up for lost time ever since that life-changing event.

Even from a distance, my instinctual interest is aroused when I see the long thin arms and legs of a shapely woman, clothed or unclothed. So many things from my preteen childhood seem to trigger my attraction to women. It's still their voices and those little gestures and movements that make them seem more delicate than men. I think it has long been imprinted into almost every man's evolutionary DNA.

■ ■ ■

Over time I have come to appreciate the difference between men's and women's sexuality. The difference is somewhat like making music with drums or violins. Men are drums, simple as a hollow log or as intense as a tight skin stretched across the frame of a snare drum. You can get a beat without the least knowledge of music and they will sound off, creating vibrations good enough to be the pulsing rhythm in a band or orchestra – this rhythmic throbbing eventually resulting in a climactic finale. No finesse, no gentle strokes, not a single musical note. They are primitive, raw, easily excited, and always eager to be part of the pounding sound that finds satisfaction in their own beat.

Women, strike me more like violins – each note teased out by the correct caress, movement of sensitive fingers along their body, in just the right spots, with affectionate touches to create the pleasure that excites every fiber of their being. The woman requires a man to use various part of his body against hers, to excite her skin in her most sensitive places. Her experience is heightened as he moves his bow at just the right angle, its movements meant to stimulate the most exhilarating responses. Moving up and down, or in and out, side to side, the bow excites her inner strings, making unique music that captures their connected passion. It takes time and practiced skills of maturity to help a woman reach a crescendo of erotic pleasure, a reward to both her and him.

I've found each woman requires touching and caressing unique to them, to experience the magnificent pleasurable release of an orgasm. For some it's a gentle touch, like butterflies landing upon her most sensitive organ, while others demand a firmer stroke to reach her full and total climactic end. On the more animalistic side of humanity, I think it just takes the sight of a naked woman to excite most men, creating a rhythmic sound within us ready to explode in sexual satisfaction with only a little encouragement from an affectionate woman. But a woman may need the considerate attention of a patient man, to make sure she achieves her pinnacle of satisfaction, before he beats his own drum.

For me, making love to a woman is not only a great pleasure, but a privilege. I get a tremendous pleasure helping to bring a woman I care about to her most enjoyable orgasm. There's even greater pleasure when that woman I'm with enjoys bringing me to my climactic satisfaction as well. I firmly believe good sex has more to do with the mental attitude of each partner rather than athletic physicality. Though there is no denying that great sex often has both. This relationship does not require a long-term monogamous relationship. It can be between dating couples, those who have few encounters, or even in more casual relationships such as "friends with benefits." While most animals are limited to their mating seasons, us humans are fortunate, we can enjoy these activities year round.

But everything in life, even sex, does not always go well, at least it hasn't for me. Years later, after college, I was living in a new three bed-room apartment in Douglaston, on Long Island. In those days I drove a red Austin Healey 3000 sports car. Things were good. I had become very comfortable with my sexuality, having had many satisfying and enjoyable relationships. I had a great apartment, subdued lighting, leather furniture, a great sound system, a cowhide area rug over wooden floors in the living room, and a Pier One straw mat by the side of my bed. I shared the three bedroom apartment with two other guys.

Something happens I have never experienced before, and it is incred-ibly terrifying. This night, I am with a beautiful girl, I'm in my mid-twenties and she is nineteen. This traumatic experience blocks me from remembering her name. We have been out a couple of times and this night she comes over to my apartment. My apartment mates are out so we have the place to ourselves.

One thing leads to another and after smoking some grass and having a glass or two of wine, we make our way to my bedroom. The lights are down low, the music soft and dreamy, everything set for what I expect to be an amazing sexual experience. She has that cheerleader body, so I am particularly excited, anticipating incredible sex. And to make it even bet-ter, she seems as enthusiastic as me.

It starts out so perfect – kissing, caressing, going slow and gentle, exciting every inch of each other's body. For me, being connected to the center of a woman's body sexually is a very powerful and special feeling. We position ourselves for that moment when our genitals will be bound together in a throbbing burst of pleasure.

Our verbal excitement, unbridled by there being no one else in the apartment, sounds like a chorus of pleasure and pain, but in a good way. I think we climax at the same time and come to a perspiring rest next to each other. I pull the covers over our spent bodies. Several minutes later she pulls off the covers, gets out of the bed. She hesitates a moment, before heading for the bathroom. She says the weirdest thing, "Something's wrong." I've never heard any girl say that before. "What? What's wrong!?" I sit up and turn up the lights. Everything looks just fine.

I pull back the covers to get up, the sheet is covered with blood. Not just a little blood, but lots of dark red blood. There are clumps of blood trailing across my Pier One straw mat and floor, behind her path to the bathroom. I'm horrified. Thoughts race through my mind, "Oh shit, she's going to die! I have to get her to the hospital before she dies! I'm going to be charged with murder, I know it! How could I have done this? Was I high on drugs and stabbed her, but I don't have a knife." I feared I'd be forever known as the first or only guy to be tied to a "death by lethal penis."

She calls from the bathroom, "I think I need to go home." I say, "We have to go to the hospital right away." But she insists I take her home. I figure she just wants to die at home. I drop her at her house, not a word spoken in the car as I sweat every mile until we get there, hoping she doesn't pass out and die in my car. When I return to my apartment I think for sure I will hear about her death on the news, that night or the next day. I clean up the blood as if it's a murder scene and I want to leave no evidence for my roommates or the police. I hated to trash that straw mat.

I can't bring myself to call her the next day, thinking her parents will answer and tell me she died. A couple of days later she calls. I am so relieved. I ask, "Are you okay?", thinking she is probably in the hospital. She confesses, "I was a virgin, that's why there was so much blood." Well shit, I think this isn't something a girl should forget to mention to a guy.

This was a first for me, and I cannot understand why any guy would want to have sex with a virgin. I've never had sex with a virgin since, so I guess all the women I've been with, thereafter, have already shocked the shit out of some poor slob along the way.

■ ■ ■

A nice, calm and respectable lady goes into a pharmacy and walks right up to the pharmacist. She looks straight into his eyes and says, "I would like to buy some cyanide, to poison my husband."

The pharmacist's eyes bug out, he exclaims, "Lord have mercy! I can't give you cyanide to kill your husband! I'll lose my license! They'll throw both of us in jail! Absolutely not, you CANNOT have any cyanide!"

The lady reaches into her purse and pulls out a picture of her husband in bed with the pharmacist's wife.

The pharmacist looks at the picture and replies, "Well now. This is different. You didn't tell me you had a prescription."

■ ■ ■

A man and his wife were making their first doctor visit prior to the birth of their first child.

After everything checked out, the doctor took a small stamp and stamped the wife's stomach with indelible ink.

The couple was curious about what the stamp was for, so when they got home, he dug out his magnifying glass to try to see what it was.

In very tiny letters, the stamp said, "When you can read this without a magnifying glass, come back and see me."

7

COUPLING: IT'S COMPLICATED

Primates regularly had sex with many different partners beginning millions of years ago, not only to increase their species, but because they liked doing it. Having perfected this practice over millions of years has had a deep-seated instinctual imprint on the human psyche. I think this history might make it more difficult for people to be perfect monogamous beings. But many societies have punished those who deviate from this social discipline which is so foreign to our natural instinct. Being naked surely contributed to promiscuity, but once humans migrated to more temperate and colder climates, sexual activity must have slowed down, when clothing was preferred to death.

Within the last 150,000 to 200,000 years, modern humans fought for territorial rights, food and living space. In the world of cavemen, brute force and violence took the best real estate; today it's money. During the ancient civilizations of Egypt, Greece and Rome, warring adversaries joined together through arranged coupling between sons and daughters. It was also quite the rage among the royal families of Europe for the sake of business, wealth and world dominance. A husband, unhappy with such an arrangement, might have reported his wife thrown from her horse, her head split open by a rock. Perhaps she would indeed be found dead from being struck by a rock, but likely in the absence of any horse's participation.

Would anyone be surprised if there were a multitude of victims from arranged marriages found dead in their nightgowns victims of hunting accidents or while cleaning their guns? These seem like crazy things from the past, but could it happen today? Recently in the news was a story about a guy who shoots his girlfriend to death, claiming to have mistaken her for an intruder breaking into their home – *from a bathroom within their house?* This makes as much sense as if he had pointed out multiple knife wounds to her back, claiming she had accidently stabbed herself to death.

Women have long chosen mates for family and security, while men take a simpler approach to mating – typically chasing the *best-looking* women, a standard that keeps changing. Today, thin – even "stand in the same place twice to cast a shadow-thin," is in vogue. Yet there are others who find women with large backsides exciting, not unlike the attraction our primate relatives have with big female rumps. Scientists know chemical messages are sent between our less developed primate relatives to attract mates from a great distance. This has not yet been demonstrated for people, but I would not be surprised, if in the future, the subconscious scent between humans contributes to attractions resulting in mates.

Where is the chemist who can demonstrate the success of such a reliable chemical scent? Maybe a company will come along selling scents designed to attract the perfect human mate based on matching their compatible genetic pheromones. Maybe the company will be called "Scentimate." Then men or women could selectively attract each other when coming into range at a party, networking event, or passing on the street.

It's probably not by chance that the human mammal, who stands erect, is the only primate who sports large breasts? I don't think anyone denies an attractive figure excites men from a distance. A few hundred years ago, voluptuous, plump, Rubenesque women were most desirable. Such a profile would immediately excite men. Don't most men still treat an attractive woman like a trophy, not unlike the primitive success of a hunt; something to show off to the other men in the "tribe"? A friend's wife sports a license plate on her car that reads, "Trophy wife." I guess she's proud of her success in landing a financially secure, older man. Wouldn't this make him her trophy, not her his?

I've wondered why most women seem to age less attractively then men? It's likely due to evolution and nature's inclination to propagate the species. Older women can't bear children after menopause, and thus nature is harsher on them than males who can have viable sperm well into old age. So men remain a little more attractive as they age, while women have a greater struggle to retain their beauty and youthful appearance. But at a certain point, nature gives up on men as well.

The "dirty old man" label might have come about because as men age, their sexual inhibitions diminish as they get closer to *no more sex forever,* which we call death. They have nothing to lose by being less politically and socially correct in pursuit of a woman's affections. They are not "dirty old men," they are just men who are now blunt and not so socially correct. Older, wiser, more experienced, and inclined to treat women better than younger men who are still exercising their virility. When people see an older man with a much younger woman, not a daughter, women think he's taking advantage of her, using his wealth or celebrity to gain her affections. Men more likely will admire the match, maybe hoping for one of their own in the future. Might it be the younger woman taking advantage of the older man for money or security, with the expectation that his expiration date is likely to occur well before hers?

And why has promiscuity favored men more than women for thousands of years? Probably because men have always had far less of a chance of getting caught. Women often broadcasted their secret rendezvous in a public and costly way, by getting pregnant. Since the time of the Roman Empire condoms have been available, allowing women to choose to be promiscuous, but requiring the full cooperation of their male partners. With the advent of birth control pills and other devices, the playing field has been leveled. Sociological studies tell us things shifted as we moved into the late 20th Century with more women engaging in sex, with more partners, while single, engaged, or married.

■ ■ ■

One summer I was a counselor at a day camp in Levittown, on Long Island. I taught at a Junior High during the school year and took this summer job to supplement my income. I met an attractive female counselor that summer and we became pretty good friends within just a couple of weeks. Wendy and I were in our mid-twenties. We wrote poems to each other and had interesting conversations, hitting it off so well I thought she could be the one for me. I pulled everything I had out of my "How to get a date toolbox," but I couldn't make it happen. Maybe always being honest with the girls and women I met and dated did me in, since more successful guys seem to use the truth more sparingly. I was still in dating-purgatory, bound to learn mostly by one failure after another. A couple of weeks before camp ended, Wendy told me the very last thing I could have imagined; she was engaged. That was bad enough, but she had been engaged since before camp began, never wearing her ring to avoid damaging it.

It's the last week of camp, she invites me to her apartment for the counselor end of summer farewell party. I get there early, before the others, and present her a small bouquet of flowers. After her engagement surprise, I make every effort to see her as just another counselor friend.

When I arrive she asks, "Would you help me out by opening the bottle of wine I have in the kitchen and pouring us a couple of glasses?" After using all my manly skills to remove the cork, totally intact, I pour two glasses of wine, figuring we are getting a head start before the other counselors arrive.

I return to the living room with a dramatic presentation, revealing to Wendy a glass of Cabernet in each hand, with a "Ta Da!" She stands before a pile of her clothing on the floor, revealing to me, also all she has, with a "Ta Da!" Right there I feel like the luckiest guy in the world. This was it, her engagement is over.

I would remember the rest of that afternoon for years. Hey, the way I looked at it, dating a girl is like trying out to be a permanent member of her team. Lots of people can try out at the same time, so I wanted my chance at bat.

But it was not to be. Wendy insisted she had her life planned. Her fiancée would have a great future working with her father and their families had known each other for years. So there I was, face to face with the poster-girl for "The Women's Sexual Freedom Movement." When I saw her on the last day of camp, it was a sad farewell for me, but I was, and still am grateful for that amazing summer we had together.

■ ■ ■

Coincidently, while writing this chapter, I had lunch with a film friend who told me about the woman he recently met while playing tennis. He sees her a couple of times a month on short text notice. Yes, *short text notice*! This would have been awfully difficult when smoke signals were the main communications tool. He doesn't have her address and doesn't even know her last name. She texts him a few days in advance so they can meet at a hotel just outside of Palm Springs. He's in his fifties, no longer married, and has no idea if she's married. But he glows when he tells me how attractive she is and that they have terrific sex. She stays for two and a half hours, not more, not less, only between 2:00 and 4:30. It's become a discreet and exciting sexual relationship outside her socially prescribed life. She wouldn't be doing this if it didn't make her life better.

Back in the 1500s, when marriage by choice came into its own, the average person lived to about fifty. It's entirely plausible that a marriage would last "until death do us part," which might be twenty or thirty years. With longevity now pushing ninety plus, maybe marriage contracts should be re-drafted. What if marriage certificates were to expire in ten years for couples without kids, renewable with mutual consent? Those with children would have a marriage certificate expire in twenty-five years, also renewable with mutual consent? In both situations there should be a fair and equitable sharing of accumulated assets during the marriage, and if appropriate, alimony and child support.

I think men marry primarily for good, regular sex, followed secondarily by what people call love, which also includes elements of sex. Almost every guy I knew who got married expected he would never again need to masturbate. If only that were true... Of course there might be the necessity for such self-satisfaction during the late stages of pregnancy, shortly after childbirth, and during occasional illnesses. A man's sexual happiness might be calculated to be indirectly proportional to how often he masturbates. As the rate of masturbation increases, the quality of the marriage is likely to decrease. While an orgasm arrived at by masturbation feels great, as most men and women can attest, fortunately, most people find it even better with another consensual partner. Otherwise, we would have masturbated ourselves into extinction.

If sex is bad or absent for a man, the likelihood of a continued marriage will be in serious jeopardy. It might also be true for some women. Hearing years of guy talk, it seems the consensus is that frequency is paramount. Of course quality should never be underestimated. A father's responsibility is to educate their sons, when they reach the appropriate age, about sex. Of primary importance is to making sure they know a woman's clitoris is not located in her vagina. I failed to educate my son with "that talk," when he reached the appropriate age. For some reason it just flashed by me before I knew it. I made up for this deficiency by providing him with an excellent illustrated book.

The first indication of a good marriage is a wife who initiates sex from time to time. Sadly, after some number of years of marriage, and particularly after having children, many women are less and less likely to initiate sex. It may become only as common as seeing a comet. Actually this is unfair, it may happen more often – let's say, "once in a blue moon." I always wanted to use this expression. A "Blue Moon" is the second full moon in any month, which only happens about once every two and half years.

Brad is one of the guys I play tennis with and part of a guy talk group. He believes wives are more sexual when they go on vacation than when they are at home. Brad says, "Wives are more apt to have sex in a new bed and new room instead of at home." I'm sure he is speaking from personal experience. Brad's concern for his friends having pleasurable vacations includes his reminder to them, "Don't forget your Viagra." For the sake of his sex life he might do well to invest in a new bed several times a year, and to improve things even more, move his bed from one room to another.

Might he be right? Does a hotel room bring a woman, as well as a man, back to their more youthful years? If a wife or girlfriend finds it troublesome to have sex in the middle of the day because it means undressing and dressing again, this is not good. I think sex should be as frequent on vacation as it is at home – if it's frequent enough. If travel somehow enhances the frequency of sex between couples, then I wish everyone more vacations, along with whatever drugs it takes.

A doctor friend at the tennis club, happened to mention before the game, that frequent sex can reduce the chance of men getting prostate cancer. Now he tells me! He cited some research he came across that having an orgasm three times per week can reduce a man's chances of having a stroke or heart attack by almost 50%. I wonder if a wife's natural inclination for less sex is possibly why men often die before their wives. So finally there's some scientific evidence for that old question, "Why do men die before their wives?"… Comically answered, "Because they want to!" How great it would be if doctors determined that frequent sex also reduces a woman's chances of contracting uterine, ovarian, or breast cancer? Maybe marriage vows would then include: "I promise to love you in sickness and in health and to have sex with you at least three times per week to protect us both from the ravages of cancer."

The second general observation that leaps from the lips at guy chats is that women, whether hetero or gay, love to be the recipients of cunnilingus at every age. Even if the woman provided fellatio pleasures to her husband before marriage, it almost universally is lost from their toolboxes over the years, until it becomes a lost art. But now I wonder if men, as they age, also lose some enthusiasm for pleasuring their partners. Humans evolved with sexual instincts and behaviors that may not be compatible with today's longer lives. Maybe this is why this crude statement has entered the male social dialogue, *"Show me a beautiful woman, and I'll show you a guy who is tired of fucking her."* This may just be a manifestation of that lingering instinct for multiple partners. Also, while crass as it may be, it could be speaking to the length of time couples are expected to stay together, as longevity far exceeds that of early modern humans. So today coupling for an extended time must depend more on personality and character. Most people will scratch their heads and wonder why so many men divorce beautiful women. I think it's much more about what's inside those beautiful heads of those beautiful women they divorce.

The third less spoken complaint in the guy chat groups is the monotony of having sex in the same way each and every time. Maybe men like different sexual positions because it substitutes for having sex with a variety of women (a subconscious primal instinctual drive). When it's always the same, it's more of a mechanical exercise than an exciting fantasy. Not that intercourse is less satisfying, but the process of getting there loses a lot of its potential eroticism. I wonder if porn for men is their vicarious way to imagine the satisfaction of their ancestral desire for sexual variety. Maybe it's helpful for couples to each have occasional safe, discreet, trusted, sexual experiences with others, to break stretches of boredom and learn new or other ways to bring sexual excitement back to their bedrooms. Books, remember them, can also be a source of suggested variety.

We all know lots of marriages end in separation or divorce. What's surprising is many guys I know who have divorced say they should have done so ten or fifteen years earlier. I wouldn't be surprised if women feel the same way. And not unexpectedly, the sex had not been very good, was infrequent, and often absent during many of those years. It's not easy to end a relationship with someone you've had many years of good times with, and with whom you've developed a friendship. If separating puts a financial burden on each partner, resulting in both having a lesser quality of life, it's nearly impossible to separate or divorce. After all is said, quality of life is what really matters, for the short time we all have left.

But even as men age, many are still focused on the fantasy of exciting sex. Men can't help it. It takes little to get them visually excited. Just looking at an attractive woman poses the question, "What's she like having sex?" While most men won't admit it, I'm convinced every man with an active libido runs this fantasy through their minds several times a day. Men are continuously vulnerable because women dress almost every day to be attractive to men. They accentuate the body parts they think are most alluring with flattering clothing and adorning themselves with jewelry.

We hear a lot about misogynists and yet, I think they represent a minority of men, so isn't it about time we had a positive word for a man who loves the females of our species? How about we use "womenphile," lover of women? There are lots of "philes," probably one for everything someone loves. There is "oenophile" – loves wines; a good match to a "turophile" – a lover of cheeses; and "pluviophile" – lover of rainy days. There is even "gynotikolobomassophile" – a person who loves nibbling on a woman's earlobes. But finally I came across "philogynist," meaning a lover or friend of women. Too close to "misogynist." I'm sticking with "womenphile."

It's been reported that as most women pass their forties or fifties, their hormonal interest in sex seems to drop off, and it's even more prevalent among women who have had children. It's a shame when either a man or woman ends up with the sex drive of a chair, leaving their partner sexually unfulfilled. This can potentially tear at the fabric of their marriage. Not many people will ever admit they have lost interest in having sex. What can be done? Sex therapy? Talking with your partner to let them know you want to have sex more than they do after you've been in a long term relationship? At some point in their life people become who they are. Wanting someone to be more sexual is like wanting someone to be more athletic. Ever try to get a non-athletic person to become really good at a challenging sport like tennis or golf?

What if the partner who has little or no interest in sex, gave their "loved one" permission, as long as they didn't get romantically involved, to have safe sex with someone else. Might this help to keep long-term marriages between friends together? Physical, protected sex, can be just an exercise, so long as it is not about emotional love and drawing away either participant from an existing marriage. Today there are services provided by women, who for a price, will provide a hug and cuddling with a male partner. I wonder why it's not considered prostitution, even though it too provides "affectionate services" for money.

■ ■ ■

From my apartment window in Italy, while attending medical school, I can see the Bologna train station plaza. It isn't long before a pattern of behavior becomes apparent. Each workday about five or six PM, a number of women gather by the side of the road, along the street, at the plaza. They are of various sizes, shapes and ages. A number of Fiat 500s, very small but efficient family cars, pull up to the plaza. Women get into cars and the driver speeds away. About an hour later, the cars reappear and women hop out, before the driver again races off, not to be seen again for a few days.

I go to my source of Italian information, Alda, our housekeeper. I call her to the window. She's a reserved woman in her mid-forties, married for twenty years with three children. She smiles as she looks down at the street. Alda speaks slowly, so I can understand what she is about to say, since she speaks no English. "This is good."

There it is, a clash between Italian values and their practical approach to life in a very Catholic country. Most American women take offense at such apparent transgressions from monogamy. But in the early years of my marriage, when I went to Brussels each month, my wife would say, "Enjoy yourself, but don't bring anything home." I was impressed and thought she was being very European. It never made me any more likely to get involved with the women I met on these trips, but it made me feel more comfortable.

These men, who drove to the plaza, did not wear masks, use unidentifiable rental cars, or any other disguises. While those with less financial means use these street-level services, the wealthier men use the more expensive call-girls or have a mistress. I never saw police interfere with these daily activities, which apparently suggested they were entirely acceptable.

Alda continues, "A man's sex drive follows him to the grave. This can break holy bonds of marriage. The man takes a woman from the street. A wife knows she'll not lose him to such a woman. Or would such a woman want him. He comes home less interested in sex. Mothers care all day for children and then their husbands. They're tired." Alda's final words, as she throws a kiss toward the plaza, "Mi Dio. Bless these ladies."

But that was then. A recent divorced female attorney friend, in her forties, told me women are changing, and changing rapidly. She said the percentage of women today having extramarital sex is equal to men. Wendy, my camp friend, could have been at the forefront of that trend, and my friend's two and a half hour texting mystery woman is a current example of this reality.

My attorney friend paraphrased from some magazine research she read that women are doing this for many of the same reasons as men – they discover the pleasure of safe, discreet, extramarital affairs, even when they are not entirely displeased with their marriage or significant other. It may be for the sake of variety, many women having only had sex with one or two people in their lives. Or to escape boredom, and even to enrich a marriage that may be getting stale.

European societies have outgrown the apparent social-sexual standards burned into the minds of Americans. Why is it that the American perception of sex has been something a women gives and a man takes, rather than a mutual exchange of pleasure – neither one the sole recipient or donor? Maybe the younger generations are becoming more European-like in thought. It's understandable why some women may seem to behave like tight-legged hockey goalies constantly guarding their nets from men. As men come at them, maneuvering with lots of charm, appealing moves, and smooth talking, women see them as only interested in driving pucks into their nets to score. No wonder they often block entry at any cost. Such a score in the past would have likely resulted in pregnancy. But things have changed. Women now have more sexual control. While still using discretion, they can lower their guard and find pleasure without being overly defensive.

An expression of a complicated relationship that can be cobbled together in modern society might be exemplified by what I call the Tracy Hepburn Syndrome. Spencer Tracy and Katharine Hepburn had a mutually beneficial loving relationship for twenty-six or twenty-seven years. Not only did they never marry, but Spencer Tracy remained married to his wife for his whole life. This relationship, among these three, seems to have benefited them all.

After some research and observations, I found pleasure drives almost everything humans strive to do or achieve, and the two pleasures on top of the list are likely sexual satisfaction and laughter. This is particularly true of men, who until they are in a permanent relationship, are driven for success to attract a woman of their choice, for the opportunity to have sex with them on a permanent or semi-permanent basis. I don't think people leave their homes for work, play, or even to go shopping, without preparing themselves to look attractive to other people sexually, whether hetero or gay. If not looking for an exciting new relationship, it's a good feeling to be admired or desired by those we meet, even if it's not mutual.

While Tracy and Hepburn personify the complexity of humans seeking sexual happiness, some people will find all they need in their marriage. Others will find it in living together or being single, while still others may need to have more complicated human relationships through some or all of their lives. We all know life takes many turns and twists, finding people in new and sometimes surprising situations, due to circumstances, often beyond personal control. I want to always be connected to people I respect, like, trust, and feel an affection for, as long as I'm here.

Mature adults realize life can be cut short due to accidents or illness; the number of years left to enjoy physical and emotional pleasures are limited. It's not surprising many more women are now willing to take the same kind of risk men have been taking since they were boys, asking girls and women out. In my experience, many more non-American women are more likely to enthusiastically ask a man out or to shower with them, without a second thought of fearing rejection. I think women will find they will rarely be turned down, and men love to be on the receiving end of such an invitation. Everyone should look to find pleasure in every day of their lives. If you want something reasonable, ask for it. If the person you ask says no, it's better than you not asking, because they may just say yes.

I was surprised to hear a doctor, during a radio interview, say that many men lose interest in sex before their wives, leaving the wives unfulfilled sexually. I read that married couples in 2015 had sex an average of fifty-five times per year, while in 1990 the average was seventy-three times. This drop could be because of more electronic distractions, or is it a national condition of lower libidos among humans? Are more women seeking to spend time with other men for discreet, safe sex, making them feel more appreciated and attractive than they feel with their current partner? Such behavior can be a better alternative to separation or divorce. Men may find the attention and affection of another woman, adds to their overall happiness without threatening their permanent relationship… the Tracy Hepburn Syndrome.

Men are likely to need to blow off steam now and then when anger in a relationship approaches hate. This may be with another woman and while it may not be socially proper, if nobody is hurt, maybe it can keep a couple together. I'm not sure women don't need to do the same thing from time to time. We live our own lives and choose to share that life with someone else, not to surrender it to them entirely. Our dreams and fantasies, among other things, are ours alone to do in our short lives. It seems some outside physical, close friendships can make coupling or marriages more manageable for women and men as they pass through various phases of life. Maybe women go through some kind of mid-life crisis like men. But for men, I think the mid-life crisis might last until death.

■ ■ ■

A lady goes to the doctor, complains her husband is losing interest in sex. The doctor gives her a pill, but warns her it's still experimental. He tells her to slip it into his mashed potatoes at dinner.

That night, she does it. About a week later, she's back to the doctor.

"Doc, the pill worked great! I put it in the potatoes like you said! It wasn't five minutes later that he jumped up, raked all the food and dishes onto the floor, grabbed me, ripped all my clothes off, and ravaged me right there on the table!"

The doctor says, "I'm sorry, we didn't realize the pill was that strong! We'll be glad to pay for any damages."

"Nah," she says, "that's okay. We're never going back to that restaurant anyway."

■ ■ ■

This man sits quietly reading his paper one morning, peacefully enjoying himself, when his wife sneaks up behind him, whacks him on the back of his head with a huge frying pan.

Man: "What was that for?"
Wife: "What was that piece of paper in your pants pocket with the name Marylou written on it?"
Man: "Oh honey, remember two weeks ago when I went to the horse races? Marylou was the name of one of the horses I bet on."
The wife looks satisfied and goes off to work around the house. Three days later as he sits in his chair reading, she repeats the frying pan swatting.
Man: "What the hell is that for, this time?"
Wife: "Your horse called."

■ ■ ■

When Henry comes back from visiting the doctor, he looks terrible. He tells his wife the doctor said he was going to die before the night was out. She hugs him, they cry a little, and Betty suggests they go to bed early to make love one more time.

They make love until Betty falls asleep, but Henry is too frightened to sleep because it is his last night on earth. He lies there in the dark while Betty snores.

He whispers in his wife's ear, "Betty, please, just one more time for old times' sake." But Betty keeps snoring.

Henry looks at his watch, leans over to his wife and shakes her hard, "Please Betty, just one more time for old times' sake!"

Betty wakes up, looks at him and says, "Henry, how can you be so selfish? It is alright for you, but I have to get up in the morning."

8

DIFFERENT TRAINS, SAME STATION

We take risks all the time. I'm not talking about gambling in casinos, racetracks, or lottery tickets. All of these are games we play, and if they go beyond entertainment, they can become dangerous addictions. I see life as a series of risks, and being selective, taking reasonable risks, is all that stands between me and avoiding costly mistakes. Many risks can be life-changing and exhilarating. I don't want to ever miss a great experience because of fear. Fear is powerful and should not be underestimated. Extraordinary experiences do not come along too often.

When I was in high school I was fearful of taking the smallest of risks, such as asking a girl to dance or going on a date, and even striking up a conversation with someone I didn't know. Like most maturing humans, I said no to myself to avoid any possible humiliation by rejection. Yet when it comes to bodily harm, most youngsters are fearless and behave as if they are immortal.

In junior high school, when I was still living in the Bronx, there were very few hills with grass, which when covered by snow made great sledding places. But we had one. We could pick up really good speed down this little hill but we had to make a sharp right turn at the bottom where it met the exit ramp of the Bronx River Parkway. A miss could mean sledding under the wheels of a car, unable to see us, as it turned off the ramp. Risk-taking at its max! Dumb, yes indeed, but I was a kid.

It wasn't until my junior year at college that I was able to unshackle myself from saying no to myself. It began with the Pineapple Princess. She was from Hawaii and I'm not sure if she was really a princess, I doubt it, but she was beautiful and among my guy friends, that's what we called her. One of the most beautiful girls at school. Someone likely to have dozens of guys chasing after her or likely to have a steady boyfriend. Perception is often our reality. It may be a false reality, but most of us will hang on to it in spite of contrary facts. I was playing pool one day in the CUB (College Union Building) with a bunch of my guy friends. I recently decided to never say no to myself again, no matter the cost. Especially if the cost might only be humiliation and not death! I was getting smarter each year. Isn't education great?

She comes up in conversation again as the most beautiful and untouch-able girl on campus. I declare before all of them, "I'm going to ask her out for this Friday night." After a round of outright laughter, serious doubt and disbelief hangs in the air, there is no actual betting, but my friends don't hold back on their verbal chorus figuring my odds of her saying yes being near zero. They base this on their certainty I will never have the "balls" to even ask the question. If I do, she will certainly say no.

She is in my Asian History class along with about 150 other students in the large auditorium. There is never a seat next to her since they are always coveted by her girlfriends. If rejection from her is to come like a dagger to my heart, I want as few witnesses as possible. In fact, none would be the right number. Two days in a row I see her in one place or another but she is never alone. I feel a little like an animal on the prowl seeking a deli-cate prey. Then by chance, there she is, walking to class alone. It's time to pounce, no witnesses. I catch up to her and instead of walking past, I slow to her speed. "Hi, we're in Asian class together. My name is Steve, if you're not busy this Friday, how about a drink or dinner together in town?" I say it and hold my breath. I imagine a considerate rejection along the lines of, "Sorry, but I already have a date." Then for her to quicken her pace away from me. She looks at me with her beautiful eyes and says, "Sure." I almost fell out of my shoes.

Can you believe it? I was shocked. So shocked I had trouble coming up with where to go and what to do. I met her at her dorm and we walked into town. We had dinner at the Pink Spot, a popular restaurant, and then went for a couple drinks at P & G's, also picked for maximum exposure – but both good places in town. She said she was rarely asked out and didn't understand why. When the more popular guys saw her out with me, she never had another open weekend night the rest of that semester. And she did end up with a regular boyfriend – the captain of the basketball team.

■ ■ ■

Sometimes I see my life as a series of train stops on an amazing journey, meeting and interacting with many people along the way. The Pineapple Princess and I shared a common station for a few hours, that one night, then our lives traveled on in separate directions. I recall a plane ride when I met a very attractive black flight attendant serving my section of the plane. I was friendly and talkative with her as I often am with most people I meet.

I stop by the bar that night at my hotel and see her sitting with a guy flight attendant. By this time in my life I rarely say no to myself, thanks in part to the Pineapple Princess. I take the seat next to them and strike up a conversation.

This was just after I received my Ph.D. from NYU so I must have been about thirty. She was a bit older, probably in her late thirties.

As we sit there, she reminds me of Diana Ross, but with her hair in a close cut Afro, with a beautiful face and great smile. To me she is the classic look of an attractive flight attendant.

I can't remember her name or even which airline it was.

We have a couple of drinks before the guy flight attendant excuses himself, she and I continue to talk. The bar area is thinning out, so not wanting to regret a missed chance to get to know her better, and to avoid later that night saying to myself, I shoulda…, I say, "Want to continue talking in my room or yours? I'll get a bottle of champagne to go." She thinks about it for what seems like minutes, then turns to me and says, "My room, but it can't be for long. I have an early flight tomorrow."

I never knew if she was engaged, married or single, it didn't come up and it didn't matter. Here we were, on trains heading in different directions, with a stop at the same station for this night.

I buy a small bottle of champagne, good for two glasses. We go to her room and talk for quite a while. She has an interesting childhood growing up in the South and going to college in Boston. She seems as interested in my life as I am in hers. We are truly from different worlds. She looks at her watch and says, "Got that early flight in the morning." I say," Okay let's just finish our champagne." She agrees and we continue to talk about college, New York, and Atlanta. I stumble into saying apparently the most powerful words of that evening, resulting in the opening of heaven.

I tell her I never kissed a black girl. She leans over to me and kisses me. It was friendly but on the lips. So in my mind it's my reward for having the self-confidence to ask her for more time together after leaving the bar. Mission accomplished! We finish the champagne and she excuses herself to go to the bathroom. She's back in a few minutes. She's still fully dressed in a white blouse and dark skirt. I stand to leave and she comes up to me; we're now standing face to face, very close. I lean in to kiss her, she kisses back and holds me tight to her body. I move my hands up and down her side then reach behind her to pull her blouse out from her skirt so I can reach her bra. My hands move up her soft smooth back to where I know a bra strap should be, but it is nowhere to be found. Good thing, because my record of unclipping bras in the heat of the moment is not very good. She steps back a foot or two from me, unbuttons her white blouse, revealing her beautiful bra-less breasts. Several years earlier this could have caused me to climax right then and there. But I have fortunately matured.

She helps me off with my shirt, she removes her blouse, then my slacks and her skirt. She has an amazing body and for a guy who had never been with a black girl it strikes me how tan she is with no tan lines or areas of white. We take off our underwear, get into bed. She has the silkiest and softest skin I had ever felt. I couldn't help but touch her everywhere and take as much of her in as I could. Her enthusiastic touching and caressing excites every inch of my body like I have never experienced before. This was like a dream and is probably helped a little by the bar drinks and glass of champagne. I'm not sure if she has ever been with a white guy, but it feels like she is making love as a representative of her race, wanting to make sure this experience will never be forgotten.

We climax together, lay in each other's arms for about a half hour. She turns, says, "It's getting late…" I know this is my cue to leave. I start to get out of bed, she pulls me back, says,"… we only have time for one more." And we do it again. Just as I get up to dress and leave, she sits up, pulls me to her for a kiss and says, "You can never again say you never kissed a black girl."

It leaves me with an amazing appreciation of sex with her that I have clearly remembered the rest of my life. It was nothing like a conquest but rather a mutually interesting and enjoyable conversation, between two people from different worlds, ending in pleasurable, safe, and consensual sex. There were no rules; we zipped ourselves out of our current lives and shared some time together. The next day we went our separate ways and never saw each other again. I can't remember her name and I'm sure she doesn't remember mine. It was a terrific experience, worth the risk society might have placed on it. Life is too short to miss such great moments. Our encounter hurt no one in our lives and yet it enriched us both.

I've often wanted to say something to a stranger, start up a conversation, maybe get to know them, because they strike me as someone who might be interesting. It could be because of their looks, the way they dress, or what they're doing. How often have you been inhibited, fearing their reaction, or feeling that societal monkey on your back telling you it's not proper? Well I no longer stand for those inhibitions. I seek out conversations regularly with strangers, and wish I had begun doing so many years ago. There are amazing people out there.

Since life is short, there is no time to waste in hoping these encounters will come around a second time, because in all likelihood they won't. I think it's a waste of a piece of life when any of us say, "I should have said something." Because it might have developed into a new friendship.

And I'm done thinking, "What would have happened if I said something or did something else?" Most all of us grow out of our youthful inhibitions and self-doubt, sooner or later, but it's harder to break away from societal restraints, and its stifling rules and standards. No more "should have," "could have," "would have," in my life! Living a life of regrets no longer have a place in my life.

■ ■ ■

I took a major risk many years ago when an opportunity arose for which I could have easily said, no thank you. I had been teaching for several years in a stable secure job I loved. Stepping out of that classroom to become a business consultant was one of those things now consistent with the evolved theme of my life, never saying no to myself. I had been playing tennis during the winter with a group of businessmen once a week at Buddy's house in Lattingtown, on Long Island. Can't play outside during the winter in New York, so we played in Buddy's house. Yes, he had two clay courts outside, and a tennis court in his house off his dining room. Ivy-covered walls, and a red clay court like you might have read about in time of the Great Gatsby. I had played tennis in college so I was still pretty good.

Walter owned eleven training facilities. One of these, in Glen Cove, next town to Lattingtown, was a mansion expanded into an executive center, and his corporate offices. It had over a hundred hotel-like rooms, lots of meeting rooms, recreational facilities, and a huge dining room and kitchen. Fortune 500 business people booked a week or two to improve their employees' skills in business management, marketing, sales, negotiations, meeting management and other business-related areas. Walter knew I was in education, with a Ph.D., so he made me an offer.

He wanted me to take a year off from teaching and work for him to determine if he could expand his business into the training component. We came to an agreed upon salary and I left the classroom. During that year I took a dozen different courses at his various facilities to evaluate the programs being offered so I could report back to Walter on how to incorporate this added element into his business. I worked from his executive offices in the mansion in Glen Cove. Of course we all kept playing tennis once a week at Buddy's. I was trained in many corporate business skills during this time. Unfortunately, I had to report to Walter at the end of the year that in almost every case the training of the executives began well before they spent time at his facilities. When they arrived at his facilities it was primarily for team building and the culmination of the skills they were being trained for over the previous several months at corporate training meetings. While I was now out of a job, one of the other guys who played tennis with us, Bob, who owned an aircraft company, was having some problems. His company built the black boxes and the radar found in the little fins you see on top and bottom of commercial airplane fuselages, as well as the radar in the nose-cones.

We talked briefly about it over tennis. His sales doubled over the past year but profits dropped. Fortunately, during my training, while researching the business for Walter, I learned how to do a "Needs Analysis" which I told Bob I could do for his company. This became my second business consulting job lasting about six months. It resulted in Bob and his partner showing increasing profits and selling their company for about five million dollars. The other player in our game, Gene, hired me to work with his son who would be taking over the family business which imported drapery textiles from Finland.

A consultant often works until they put themselves out of work and then has to find another job. Had I not taken that initial risk with Walter I would not have had about ten years of consulting work including being an investment banker, during which I became a commercial real estate broker, with licensing which I have now used for over forty years. During those ten years as a consultant I served as president of a robotics company until they were sold, and consulted for a Belgium investment firm, financing processing plants in French-speaking Africa. Life can provide interesting turns and twists, and taking reasonable risks can make this life an amazing experience while meeting fascinating people along the way.

■ ■ ■

Adam moped around all day in the Garden of Eden. God finally says, "Adam, what's up with all this moping?"

Adam tells God he is lonely. God says, "I can fix that, no problem. I'll make a partner for you. She will be called "woman.""

God tells Adam, "This woman will collect your food, cook it, and care for all your needs and wants. She will agree with all your decisions and not question your authority as head of the family."

God also says, "She will bear your offspring, and not bother you in the middle of the night if the kids wake up and cry.

"She will never nag you and will admit when she is wrong. She will also freely give you love and passion whenever you need it."

Adam says, "Wow, that's a great partner! What is this woman-person going to cost me?" God replies, "An arm and a leg."

Adam thinks for a minute, then asks, "What can I get for a rib?"

And the rest is history.

■ ■ ■

The morning after:

She: Honey, would you like me to bring your coffee to bed?

He: No, darling, I will come to have breakfast with you.

She: Would you like to have scrambled eggs, my love?

He: Sure, Kitty, two eggs, please.

She: Wait, you don't remember my name either, do you?

9

RISK VS REWARD: SOMETIMES TAKING A LEAP PAYS OFF

Some risks can't be avoided while others grab our attention. It was my junior year in college, my college friend Danny, also from Long Island, put me on the path to one of the most exhilarating experiences of my life. His whole family were true adventurers. One early summer morning, that would be 4:00 AM, Danny taught me to surf off Long Beach on Long Island. This wasn't the amazing adventure but it kind of began here. We went surfing several times that summer; it was great. He had been surfing around the world since he was little, mentored by his brothers and sisters. He was the youngest of six kids. I was the first-born in my family, so there was nobody cutting an adventurous path for me. It was up to me to create one for my three brothers.

Danny was also a great skateboarder, but he definitely had a streak of "Crazy" that was beyond my understanding. One day he rode his skateboard down the middle of a country road in hilly Huntington, L.I. After careening down one hill he rose up this next hill, blind to oncoming cars heading in the opposite direction. This worked well for him many times, as the road was not frequently travelled. But one day, he came up that hill, and while airborne, like a bug hitting a windshield, he and a car met. He broke his leg and wrist. As soon as the leg cast was removed he was back on his skateboard, wrist still in the cast, but not back on that road. He was a bit crazy, but not stupid! Today he is a patent attorney in San Antonio.

It was Danny again who took me on what I thought was the craziest leap into the world of adventure I could imagine. Danny's older brothers and sisters were avid skydivers and each, including Danny, had hundreds of jumps. His sister and her husband had sport-jumped over Vietnam in the fifties. Later, when one of his brothers was in the paratroopers during the Vietnam War, he belonged to a group called HALO. This stood for "High Altitude, Low Opening," which meant they jumped from planes at over 10,000 feet above the ground, then opened their chutes seconds before hitting the ground to avoid being picked off by enemy fire or being captured.

So you guessed it, Danny convinced me to give it a try, sports skydiving, not HALO. We went to a local dirt airfield in Gardner, NY, near our college. He and about a dozen other skydivers jumped there several times every weekend.

Danny insists on giving me the most professional training for my first jump. He has me jump off the table they use to fold the parachutes so I can practice a roll when I hit the ground. This practice is rigorous; I do it twice. He says, "The landing will be no more of an impact than jumping from a height equal to the top of a doorway." Well I don't know about you, but for me, jumping from about seven feet off the ground seems hurtful.

Then, not to miss a thing in his comprehensive training program, he has me hold on to the strut of the Cessna 150, a high-wing plane, while it sits on the field runway, with one foot on the wheel and the other on the step. He shows me how to hold the strut with both hands and prepare to push off the plane backwards, arching my body, with arms and legs spread out. He takes a few minutes to explain how pulling down on the toggles of the chute, once it opens, will change my direction and ultimately guide me to the landing site. The preferred landing area is an open field about fifty yards off to the side of the runway. I will soon find out that landing safely on this field is not as easy as it sounds when it rolls off Danny's tongue.

Danny points in each direction around the small dirt airfield, from the place I am supposed to land, after leaping from the plane. He says,

"See over there, that's the river. If you have to land there okay, but it's not a good place, it's cold and you can drown if the chute wraps over and around you.

"And over there," he points left, "that road is busy, don't land there, you'll probably get hit by a car.

"Now look there," he points right of the field, "definitely do not hit those powerlines. There is no chance if you do. You'll be electrocuted as soon as you touch them. Okay, ready to go?"

The Cessna 150 is not big. It holds the pilot, who doesn't look much like a pilot; no uniform, wearing jeans, a torn tee-shirt, and sporting a backwards baseball cap. He looks like he's in his late twenties, so he does not ooze tried and true decades of flying experience. Trish and another skydiver squeeze into the back seat, their chutes on their backs and their emergency chutes on their chests, facing forward.

Then there is me, sitting on the floor next to the pilot, where the seat used to be, facing backwards, directly at Trish, a pretty girl, in her thirties who had many jumps and who today is my jumpmaster. Trish asks, "Who packed your chute?" I tell her Danny did. She and the guy next to her share a smile, causing a ripple of nervous energy to race through my spine. Trish then says, I guess to provide some kind of calming effect, "He's probably the fastest parachute packer here." Today I'm not looking for "fastest." I'm much more interested in the "best."

Our cowboy pilot calls out, "We're off." He revs up the engine and taxies to the end of the relatively short runway. By the way, there is no door on my side. They take it off to make it easier for jumpers to exit the plane. The plane races down the dirt runway, bouncing along, then sharply turns skyward to avoid the stand of large maple trees at the end of the runway. Trish holds my "static line" coming from the back of my parachute back-pack. It's attached to five pins along the backpack which when pulled, like a ripcord, will open the parachute pack and a little "pilot chute" will pop out. Well it's supposed to pop out! This is called a static line jump and I will not be responsible for pulling a ripcord to open the main chute.

When I'm about fifteen feet below the plane, the static line will run out, which will be clipped to the underframe of the pilot's seat. It will then rip out these five pins and out should come that pilot chute followed by the main chute. If the main chute does not open, then I have a ripcord I must pull on the small safety chute on my chest. While I'm told this chute will likely prevent me from dying on impact, it might be equivalent to a landing off a one-story building. There is a possibility of serious damage, but I'm told it's unlikely to kill me. That is so reassuring, right?

When my body hurls toward Earth, the pilot chute is supposed to catch the air and pull out the main chute, if all goes as planned. I must be in the right position falling, "spread eagle," but not too perfect, or an air pocket will form and the pilot chute could stay next to my backpack without catching the air. This will not be good. If I go into a roll as the main chute opens, it will likely wrap around my body, preventing me from being able to open the safety chute on my chest. Danny masterfully instructs me on this point by saying, "Don't roll as you fall." That's the end of his comprehensive skydiving course. Trish reaches over, clips the end of my static line to the frame of the pilot's seat, which they expect will remain in place after I leave the plane. It wouldn't be funny if I pull the pilot's seat out with me when I jump.

Danny emphasizes his final bit of critical advice before I head to the plane. "If you don't remember anything else I tell you today, this is the most important thing you must do." Trish even repeats it moments before she tells me to get out, "Remember, you must count one-one thousand, two-one thousand, three-one thousand, then turn your head and look up to see if your chute opened. If it hasn't opened, YOU MUST PULL THE RIPCORD ON THE SAFETY CHUTE ON YOUR CHEST." Well this seems pretty simple. Count to three, a piece of cake.

The pilot flies over the airfield at the altitude I will exit the plane and drops a long ribbon with a small weight at the end. He flies around, watches where it lands. This tells him about how far and in which direction the jumper, me, must exit the plane in order to land near the field, based on current wind velocity and direction. If there are no surprise winds or parachute malfunctions, and I exercise reasonable control of the parachute, I should be on track to land on or near the airfield. After Danny's chat about the surrounding hazards, just landing near the field may not be good enough. I will go out at about 3,500 feet and the plane will then go up to about 5,000 feet for Trish and her friend to do their jump.

The pilot lines up the plane for my jump run. He turns to me, a can of soda in one hand and says, "Thirty seconds to go." He cuts the engine back to idle. Trish tells me to get out, one foot on the wheel. OOPS... my foot rolls off the wheel and I almost fall out of the plane on my back, the absolute wrong way to exit. Trish grabs my shoulder strap and keeps me from falling entirely out the door. The pilot chuckles and says, "Sorry, forgot to lock the wheels. Okay, you're good to go now." This starts to feel a little like I'm in a clown car, but it's really high up off the ground.

I test the wheel to make sure it's definitely locked before putting my weight on it again. I move my other foot out the door and onto the step while I slide both hands along the strut that rises from beneath the plane to the underside of the wing. It's very windy because of the speed of the plane, even though the propeller is at minimum rotation. As I go through these steps and look down 3,500 feet, through empty air, to the ground way far below me, many things race through my mind. Some of which include:

> I love living… what the hell am I doing?
> What if Danny messed up my chute?
> I can't quit… can't get back in… I want to… I can't.
> I don't want to die… this is crazy… I really don't want to die.

When I reach maximum falling velocity, if my chute doesn't open, I will be going about 120 MPH when I hit the ground. No chance of survival. Even hitting the river would be like slamming into concrete. Trish has to shout for me to hear her over the prop and wind noise, "JUMP!"

I JUMP!... Push off the wing strut, get right into the arched position. Look out and down and feel like I'm floating. There is no sensation of falling. Really! None whatsoever. It feels like I'm just hanging in mid-air, motionless, except for the air rushing by my face as if I'm still looking into the prop wind. It seems like I've been hanging out here for a long time, but it's only been several seconds. Of course I forget only one thing…TO COUNT. What an idiot!

When I turn my head and look up, I see the plane, but it seems like it's falling away from me, except it's me falling toward Earth, away from the plane. Then the chute opens and jerks me to what feels like a full stop. A bunch of leaves and twigs fall from the chute as it opens. I know this is due to Danny's masterful chute-packing skills. Most skydivers use the long table at the airfield to pack chutes, specifically to make sure no debris gets wrapped up in them. But now I recall Danny saying, "You have to get on the next flight and I couldn't wait for my turn at the table, but don't worry, I found a clean area to fold up your chute." Apparently it wasn't as clean as he thought.

Once the chute opens I'm hanging in the harness supported only by these very long, thin, nylon strings going up to the thin material in the shape of a parachute. They are the only things keeping me from falling to my death. I move my feet back and forth in the air. It's a unique experience, not being earth-bound, an experience I've never had. The only sound I hear is the swishing sound of air rushing by my ears as I gently glide to Earth. I can see the horizon in every direction.

I reach up, just above my head, and grab a toggle in each hand. When I pull on the right one the chute turns right and I feel like I'm moving in that direction. All the rectangular and square areas of land, bound by roads, look like an afghan lying on the Earth. The river shimmers with reflected light among the patches of land as it meanders among their geometric patterns. It's fall and the colors are amazing. I rotate all around and try to find the several areas of death Danny warned me to avoid. Most importantly I try to find the airfield. Once I think I have sighted it, I use the toggles to keep heading in the right directions.

A crow glides by at eye level in complete silence. Bet it's wondering, "What the hell is he doing up here?" The left toggle takes me to the left and does not require very much of a pull. I keep floating, floating so gently, turning to keep the airfield in sight as I hang above Earth. Then as I get within a couple of hundred feet of the ground it comes up way too fast. THUD… I strike the ground so suddenly, the forward momentum of the chute helps me go into a roll, which I also forgot to do, sprawling me out on the ground. Oh yeah, my practice jump off the table with Danny was to show me how to roll when I hit the ground so I wouldn't break my leg. It worked, my legs are intact. Yes, you heard right, the ground, just off the side of the runway, not the river, not the road and definitely not the powerlines.

I'm alive! Nothing seems broken as I hold the earth, motionless for several moments, thankful I'm here. Truthfully, I love this experience. Part of me wants to do it again, and part of me feels like I just cheated death. Danny rushes over to see if I'm okay since I'm not moving, just hugging the ground. He shares one of his dear old Asian sayings that go something like this, "You only live twice, when you are born and when you face death." I don't remember the first one, but I definitely feel like I just faced death.

I jumped two more times over the next few weeks. Was it a risk to sky-dive? Hell yeah! But it was worth every exciting, frightening, and exhilarating moment. Danny used to sit around telling the guys at college that skydiving was safer than the drive to and from the airport. But we all knew him and he had a tendency to minimize any dangers for the things he loved doing. Several weeks after my last jump a skydiver at the Gardner airfield, a friend of Danny's, crashed to Earth; a faulty chute deployment.

■ ■ ■

There are many risks in life that are unavoidable. Skydiving and mountain climbing are risks of choice, not for everyone. But I'm most impressed by all of you readers who are the real risk-takers, taking one of the most frightening risks I could imagine, far more dangerous than either skydiving or mountain climbing.

The skydiver packs his chute, takes all precautions to assure minimum risk and is not likely to run into another skydiver on his way down. We all get out on the road, at relatively high speeds, and must depend on the other drivers heading toward us to keep on their side of a LINE. That's right, not a barrier, not a moat, just a damn line. Now imagine how that risk increases when you add to the equation night, wet roads, drinking, drugs, a heart attack, a stroke, or someone having a really bad day, and for any one of a number of reasons, maybe not wanting to live another one! What if you're traveling at 40 MPH at the same speed as the oncoming car on the other side of the line, and their left front tires blows, causing their car to swerve into your lane. Talk about risk.

I was driving the other day on Sepulveda Drive in Encino, a slightly curvy road that has two lanes going in each direction, separated by a double yellow line. Have you ever noticed how "invincible" those yellow lines are in every town, city or state. No matter how thickly painted they are, do you find comfort in them being able to keep oncoming traffic from crossing over, preventing high speed head-on collisions? I haven't either. If two cars heading in opposite directions, at only sixty 60 MPH collide, the effective speed of the collision would be about the same as if you hit the Earth, traveling at maximum velocity of about 120 MPH. Sound familiar? Not a good chance of survival. Talk about risk taking, not just a few times a years but probably many times a week. Good news! On some roads, your protection is doubled by there being two sets of double yellow lines, not just one. Doesn't this make you feel doubly protected and safer?

■ ■ ■

A group of pensioners discuss their medical problems at the Day Centre over morning coffee.

"Do you realize," says one, "my arm is so weak I can hardly hold this coffee cup."

"Yes, I know." replies the second. "My cataracts are so bad I can hardly see to pour the coffee."

"I can't turn my head," rejoins the third, "because of the arthritis in my neck."

"My blood pressure pills make me dizzy," comments the fourth, adding, "I guess that's the price we pay for getting old."

"Well, it's not all bad," pipes up the first. "We should be thankful we all can still drive."

■ ■ ■

When I die, I want to go peacefully like my Grandpa did, in his sleep – not screaming, like the passengers in his car.

■ ■ ■

One guy asked the skydiving instructor, "If our chute doesn't open, and the reserve doesn't open, how long do we have until we hit the ground?"

Our jump master looked at him and in perfect deadpan answered, "The rest of your life."

Dad.

Fred.

Doug & Josh.

Debra.

Josh.

Heinz Meng & Red-tailed Hawk.

Rick.

Harry watching squirrel.

Mom and me.

Ronnie and me.

10

BEING HAPPY: IT'S WORTH THE EFFORT

I believe there's absolutely no value in worrying. *I don't worry about anything.* If I have a concern about something that affects me directly, I either deal with it – or forget it. If worrying helped, then I'm sure there would be a course at universities titled, "How to be a Good Worrier." There is no such course.

Lao Tzu, the father of Taoism, lived round 500 BC. His philosophical statements are often quoted. Some of the best-known include: *"A journey of a thousand miles begins with one step"*; and *"Being deeply loved by someone gives you strength, while loving someone deeply gives you courage."* But I find this one to be the most powerful in following my path to happiness: *"If you are depressed, you are living in the past. If you are anxious, you are living in the future. If you are at peace, you are living in the present."*

Whenever my mind goes to the past, thinking about a bad decision or missed opportunity, I try to refocus on the present. It's not easy. My mind finds it less challenging to beat me up over past mistakes. I think about how I could have done something differently, said something differently, or taken a different path than I did. All of which is of no value since I can't change what has already happened. This reminds me of what Leonardo da Vinci observed, *"In rivers, the water that you touch is the last of what has passed, and the first of that which comes."* When actors go out on their first auditions they often experience "actor's remorse." The actor thinks about what they could have, or should have done differently to have been cast in that part. Seasoned actors are able to leave an audition and not think about it again. I want to learn from past mistakes, but to dwell on them can only get me depressed. I'm sure we all are destined to continue to make mistakes throughout our lives, so I try to make my mistakes smaller, and not to repeat those I've made before.

Something as simple as a tennis match can have my mind going back to specific moments in the game, thinking how I should have played a point differently. Lao Tzu was right, this is depressing. It takes an effort to drop such thoughts. Now when I discover I've made a mistake, and a problem confronts me that has a continuing negative effect, I look for a way to deal with it rather than dwell on my misfortune. I correct it as best as I can, and as soon as possible. Surprisingly enough, it often helps. Sometimes it helps a lot. Whenever I now start to fall back on past mistakes I ask myself, "What can I do today to make things better?"

Many people seem to think writers, who spend hundreds of hours alone at a computer writing and re-writing their scripts or books, are not actually working, because they like writing. Every writer can tell you it's hard work, really hard work, even though we find joy and a challenge in this process of creation. Anyone who doesn't think so, should take one hundred blank sheets of paper and fill them with a story, the dialogue for every character, and descriptions of every different scene location in a film. But also making it enjoyable, interesting, exciting, and a thoughtful read.

■ ■ ■

I wrote a feature script with my friend Martin, based on a true story about a slave who became a charioteer, bought his freedom, and went on to become the first multi-million dollar celebrity athlete in the world. We needed to get the script sold, produced, then distributed. Even saying this quickly does not make it easy in Hollywood.

Charioteer, a "period piece," would likely cost over one hundred million dollars to produce. This was clearly a large problem. Not everyone can get such a film made. Martin and I tried to reach every potential producer, directly or indirectly, through everyone we knew who might have even the remotest connection to a producer or studio. We knew that director Ridley Scott had done the film Gladiator. We fancied our script to be "Gladiator on Wheels." How to get it to Mr. Scott became my intense focus.

I called his office. His receptionist told me, as she tells almost everybody, they do not accept unsolicited scripts and will only accept a script from an agent, manager, or attorney. I asked her who my agent should ask for when he calls back. She told me it would be Marissa. I did not have an agent. I called back a couple days later and asked for Marissa. I was put directly through to her office. "Marissa, thanks for taking my call. We have written a script we are confident Ridley would like to see. Can I get it over to you?" There was an uncomfortable silence.

"Have your agent send me a synopsis, not the script, just a synopsis." Okay, I was making a little headway. A few days later I emailed her the synopsis and said, "Marissa, my agent is traveling and is out of town. He asked me to forward this synopsis to you. I hope this is okay." Weeks went by. I thought I blew it by using my phantom agent approach. It was about a month later before I heard back from Marissa.

Her email said, "Hi Steve, Have your agent send the script over and we will have a read! Thanks!" Whoa, getting the Vice President of Production for Scott Free Productions to read our script. This unto itself was worth celebrating in a town where first-time writers must scale walls, cross barb wire, traverse moats, just to get the ear of a decision-maker in Hollywood. I sent her the script and said, "Sorry, but my agent has extended his trip with his family and asked if you don't mind me sending you the script, he will call you as soon as he returns to L.A."

A week later I receive this email: "Steve, Thank you for sending us Charioteer. You and Martin wrote a solid piece of work but unfortunately this is not something we can consider at this time. We feel this is close to Gladiator in its execution (and we are shooting Robin Hood now, which has a similar feel)." Our hopes were dashed as has happened to so many writers. However, we kept up our efforts to find a production home for Charioteer.

About a month later I get a call from Marissa. "Ridley read your script and would like you and Martin to come in to our offices for a meeting." Amazing, could this be us striking gold? We met that day at 3:00 in the Scott Free offices but just with Marissa for about an hour. She asked about all the other work we had written and asked us to send some of them to her. She said Ridley liked what he read but didn't want to do another period piece at this time, but that if we got an A-listed actor interested in playing the lead, he would *consider* directing. This meeting and the almost-success we had was something we will always remember, since not many writers ever get this far.

Years later our script was optioned by a production company to be made into a TV series, but the option expired without the company producing the show. We got to keep the $15,000 in option money they paid us and now have the script rights returned to us to find another producer. Martin went on to write several other scripts he has been trying to sell, and I wrote and produced two award-winning short films. Garry Marshall, with whom I would have co-produced a reality show, which didn't happen because his producer would not let our winner appear in this last film, "Mother's Day," paid half the cost of the premier of my second film at his theatre. I also produced a musical comedy. This was a stage show with twelve actors and singers, which was performed for its full six week run in North Hollywood to very good reviews and big audiences. An amazing experience. I have recently been paid by a novel author to co-write a script of his book and we are in the process of getting it funded to make the film. Martin and I are still searching for that right company for Charioteer. Giving up is not in our DNA.

■ ■ ■

Writing with Martin at times was difficult and yet sometimes exhilarating. It was worth the struggle of give and take, for the outcome I believe was a really good script. Not sure I would do it again, but I'm glad we did Charioteer together. This working relationship was not a bad experience, but I have heard of others who weren't as lucky. Getting into a bad business or personal relationship can happen, but I think getting out of it sooner than later results in a happier life, even if the temporary results are difficult and uncomfortable. I liken it to a bridge washed out on a road trip – a way around the problem must be found. A life without obstacles to overcome is not as fulfilling as a life in which we have such conquests along the way.

Many years ago I began to do business with a guy named Jim. He came recommended so I expected we would be doing lots of real estate deals together through his and my contacts, with the potential to double my income. Around that time my mother had a studio apartment in New York City my youngest brother had used when going to NYU but was no longer using. She was debating whether to rent it or sell it. It's always good to hold NYC real estate because over time it appreciates. Jim said he was planning on moving and would love to rent the apartment at the then-current market rent. We executed a lease with Jim, he moved in. Over the next two or three months our business was growing, everything looked great. To boot, my mother had a little income over the cost of the apartment and could hold onto it for its appreciation.

Around the fourth month, Jim missed a rent payment. He had what seemed like a reasonable excuse and promised to make it up the following month. He did not. Nor did he make any payments for the next three months. This meant my mother would have to carry the cost of the apartment – taxes, common charges, and mortgage payments. So I covered the shortfall for her.

I was also working as a consultant with Jean Claude in Brussels at the time and thought about his cardinal rule in business: "If you're not comfortable with the people, don't be distracted by the business. No matter how good it seems, in the end, the final outcome will not be good." I helped my mother file an eviction notice and terminated my business relationship with Jim. It was hard to give up what I thought would be very good additional income, but it was the right thing to do. After the dust settled, my mother sold the condo apartment, put the money in her account, and I closed the chapter of doing business with Jim.

■ ■ ■

On the more human side of life's trials and tribulations, having a child seems like an easy thing to do. After all, so many people are doing it and there's no test required to have one. Also there's so much pleasure in getting it started. But for many would-be parents it's incredibly difficult or impossible. We wanted to have two children, a boy and a girl. Having our son took five years and several medical procedures; it was difficult. What am I saying? Yes it was difficult for me, but it was horrific for my wife, Ronnie. She had to undergo a number of very uncomfortable procedures and then several miscarriages. Her pregnancy was deemed high risk right up to delivery. In fact, they had to induce labor because our son had his umbilical cord wrapped around his neck. If not helped to an early delivery, he likely would have died in the womb.

A few years after Josh was born, my wife found out she could no longer have any more children, so we decided to adopt. It would give Josh a brother or sister and this other child a brother. We applied to China and Korea. Unfortunately at that time, they deemed us too old. We were around forty. Disappointing. We turned to a highly recommended local attorney who handled legal adoptions. It was going to be more expensive, but we felt it was worth it, for a child in need of a home and a home in need of another child. It was the right thing to do. Also, when we are gone, having crossed over our respective finish lines of life, it would be good for each child to have a sibling with whom to share their lives in our absence.

The day before we were to get that baby boy, after several months of waiting and regular communications with the attorney, we got a call that the mother, who already had four children, had decided to keep this previously unwanted child. It would have been easy to ask, "Why us?" even though this is how we initially felt. "Why not us?" is as valid a question, when life takes an unexpected turn. Well the bad news is, Josh has no brother, but the good news is, this child is not homeless but is with his own parents, brothers and sisters. Life has many turns and twists. Most seem to work out pretty okay, given enough time. More often than not, I'm fatalistic, willing to accept some things as being the way they are and just dealing with them. That's life...

■ ■ ■

We're not entirely subject to life happening to us. Often we can have a hand in making it better. I've found routine and tedious things can be made more fun and thus add more pleasure to life, and *pleasure is happiness.*

Back to my college days, in that house off campus I shared with four guys... The eldest in the house, Bob, liked to cook. He had no problem cooking dinner for all of us each night when he didn't have an early evening class. However, he definitely did not like cleaning up. None of us wanted to clean pots, plates, glasses, silverware, and then have to take out the garbage.

There was no dishwasher, unless you counted one of us. Even when Bob didn't cook, he was not into cleaning up. So he introduced us to "Oollie." It's a simple game with the loser ending up cleaning the kitchen after dinner, or doing some other undesirable chore around the house. We laughed it up when we would "Oollie," making something unpleasant enjoyable, even pleasurable, especially when we won. We would "Oollie" every time there was something nobody wanted to do.

We used coins – matches worked as well, in fact any three things small enough to fit in your closed hand worked. The four of us, when Bob had cooked, he didn't have to play, would put three coins behind our backs, and then bring forward one closed hand with either one, two, three, or no coins. You could play with any number of people. With many players, the first one to guess the right total won the valued prize or benefit. On a ski trip it was this person who got the private room rather than the bunkbeds.

Each of us, going in a clockwise direction, would guess how many total coins there were in the four fisted hands. There could be no more than twelve and no fewer than none. Whoever, guessed correctly on that round was out, and definitely off cleaning-KP for that night. If there was no correct guess, we all rearranged the coins behind our backs, moved to the next person in the clockwise direction, and started off the next round of guessing. This went on until only two guys were left with up to six coins total. They kept going until one of them guessed the correct total, the other guy ended up with the chore.

It was challenging to figure out what was going on in each other's mind before calling out a total, especially when it was down to just one on one. Bob said some people can read the minds of their opponents, giving them a distinct advantage. He of course counted himself as one of those gifted people. Without question, Bob had us novice "Oollie" players figured out and often won. But by second semester, he too was doing chores he'd rather not have to do. Anyone who tries this simple game will quickly appreciate its intellectual challenge.

Laughing deserves more credit for human health. I love a funny movie, play, and a good joke. Laughter is a pleasure enjoyed by all people no matter what country, what religion, or what ethnicity. Maybe it's not just a human thing. I wonder if animals laugh as well. It is also universal no matter what the circumstances, whether at a wedding, a guy's night out, a hospital or even during war or among people in fear of losing their lives.

Finding humor in the face of death was called "gallows humor" by Freud. He used an example of such humor with a man about to be shot by a firing squad who is asked if he wants a last cigarette. *"No thanks," he replies, "I'm trying to quit."* He points out that this joke allows the doomed man to reverse the emotional control of the situation. I was surprised to hear that Holocaust survivors told of people in concentration camps finding ways to laugh from time to time. I can't imagine this, but it's apparently true.

■ ■ ■

"The Gestapo is about to shoot some Jews when the commanding officer walks up to one of them and growls, "You almost look Aryan, so I'll give you a chance. I wear a glass eye, but it's not easy to tell. If you can guess which eye it is, I'll let you go.""

Immediately, the Jew answers, "The left one!"
"How did you know?" asks the Gestapo commander.
The Jew replies, "It looks so human."

■ ■ ■

"A prisoner accidentally bumps into a Nazi guard. The guard turns and shouts, "Schwein!" (which means "pig" in German).

The prisoner bows and says, "Cohen. Pleased to meet you."

11

CRITICAL THINKING: IT MATTERS

I don't believe the statement, "Knowledge is Power." If I know cigarette smoking causes cancer, but do nothing about stopping my smoking habit, what have I achieved? A big nothing. The statement only makes sense to me when we say, "*Applied* knowledge is Power." If I learn something new and apply that knowledge, then it is truly empowering. I think many people are not thoughtful enough before making important or critical decisions. It's better to take the time to make a good decision than to decide quickly and make a bad one. As an example: A guy goes into a sporting goods store, buys his kid a bat and a ball which cost a dollar and ten cents. If the bat cost one dollar more than the ball, what is the cost of the ball? A quick, less thoughtful answer will likely be wrong.

I'm surprised how many well educated people are fooled by commercial marketing and corporate advertising. A very smart professional friend spent money on a service that "researched" his family tree. Afterwards, he proudly told us they found he was related to a famous early American signer of the constitution. I'm sure he wasn't making this up, but he was just telling us what he was told by the service he had paid. It made him feel good that he had important relatives in his past. But whoa! … Really?

Maybe I'm just a natural skeptic, but I don't think much about that family-tree research business. It's first and foremost a "business," naturally motivated by revenues and profits. What if they provide a paid customer with results that find they are related to swindlers or crooked politicians instead of prominent families? Would that customer promote their company to his or her friends? Every company wants satisfied customers to promote their services? Based on the results they provide, after supposedly "researching" a family tree, reporting a famous or interesting result is just good marketing. Some of it could be true. *Maybe.* Do their customers seek the truth? Is anyone fact-checking this information they have paid this service to deliver? I don't think they care if the results are accurate so long as it makes them proud and they get the perceived value with a good story to share with friends and family.

Critical thinking seems to be a diminishing human process among the masses. Educating students in the ways of critical thinking has been substantially diminished due to the implementation of "No Child Left Behind." This legislation emphasized memorization and feeding back facts on standardized tests, rather than developing critical thinking skills which are much more difficult and time-consuming to test.

At the University of Bologna I experienced how Italian universities evaluate students. It did not involve multiple choice and true-or-false questions, which all leave lots of room for guessing. In my biochemistry class we were given four pages at the beginning of the course with forty questions, each with two or three sub-questions. We were told our final exam would be to answer three of these forty multi part questions. Easy enough, right?

Well yes, easy enough if I could have picked the three questions. And yes, if the Professor picked the three questions, allowing me to prepare the answers at home and present my completed exam a few days later. But noooooooooo! This university has been doing this form of testing for hundreds of years and they were not about to change because they could now run simple answers through a computer to grade exams.

On the day of our final exam in biochemistry, students file into a mini-amphitheater lecture room. They take seats in the rising sections facing the front of the room where the Professor sits behind a desk. On the opposite side of his desk is an empty chair.

One by one each student is called to sit in that chair and is provided a copy of the four pages originally given to us at the beginning of course. The Professor asks, the student, of course in Italian, as an example, "Tell me about number twenty-three." As the student answers, the Professor interrupts, probes the student's answer to further ascertain his or her thorough understanding. After exhausting that questions, the professor asks to hear the answers to two more, maybe questions number fourteen and number three on that forty multiple part question sheet.

This is a slow process, but it's thorough, and to pass each course the students must have truly understood the subject matter. It is not based on being a good test taker and eliminating possible wrong answers to achieve a passing grade. I'm convinced American students need to develop good learning skills, become better critical thinkers, to become better prepared in the world today. Oh, the answer to that question is the ball cost five cents and the bat cost one dollar and five cents.

■ ■ ■

One of my favorite people in history is Leonard da Vinci. I first became fascinated by his incredible talent and work in my ornithology (study of birds) class in college which was taught by Dr. Heinz Meng. Dr. Meng raised and saved peregrine falcons and red-tailed hawks. I would often go out with him on Saturdays to a large field where he would "fly" his birds. He would let them go to fly, take out a price of meat once they were high in the sky, put it on his glove and wave his arm. They always came back to him. It was amazing to watch them fly and glide effortlessly through the air. Sometimes there would be a flock of pigeons and the falcon or hawk would catch one of them, land nearby, begin eating it until it was picked up by Dr. Meng a couple minutes later. A Peregrine Falcon can reach a speed of about 240 MPH. Leonardo studied bird anatomy and drew designs of their wings and anatomy. Both for the sake of his own knowledge and to consider what he learned to adapt it for possible human flying machines. The exact physics he discovered is used today to build our planes. He was a master of using shadows and light to make his paintings and drawings seem three dimensional.

Flying became something I wanted to experience. I found a guy who gave flying lessons at a dirt field, in Gardner, New York, near our college. He had a 1930's two seater, "Rag-Wing (fabric covered wings and body) Taildragger" (no rear wheel, a piece of metal that drag the tail along the ground) Piper Cub J-5, high wing plane. This was the same airfield a year or two later I would be skydiving at with Danny. My instructor was now an old guy who flew mail in New York during WWII. This plane had a "Joystick," no steering wheel, just this stick between my legs. I would push it forward to do down, pull back to go up, move right, while using the pedals to control the wings and tailfin to go right, and move the left pedal and joystick to go left. All these controls were done with wire cables connecting the joystick and pedals with the various parts of the wings and tail of the plane. It was fun and empowering.

However, it was noisy and most of the time I was practicing take-offs, which were easy, and landings, more dangerous and not so easy. Also from time to time my instructor would cut the engine to idle, this caused the plane to lose altitude. I would have to find an area on the ground I could glide to for an emergency landing if it was a real lost engine problem. So I found a better way to experience Dr. Meng's predatory bird experiences. I went to the Wurtsboro airport, also not too far from school, and took lessons flying glider planes. It was a way I could come closer to experiencing what it would be like to soar like a peregrine falcon or red-tailed hawk.

I arrive at the small, paved, one runway airport and get seated in the front seat, my instructor is behind me. There is a rope hooked to the front-bottom of our glider coming from the rear of a Cessna power plane about one hundred feet ahead of us on the runway. The glider is made of very thin aluminum and of course there is no engine. We are in an enclosed bubble cockpit. Someone from the airport crew picks up the right wing of our plane which lies on the ground. He levels the two wings to prepare for take-off. The Cessna powers up, takes off down the runway with us in tow.

It lifts off the tarmac and we do as well. At about 3,000 feet I pull a lever between my feet, the tow line disconnects from our plane, we are now gliding free. Like a bird we make large circles in the air to be lifted by warm air thermals rising off the side of the mountains around Wurtsboro.

It is so quiet up there, the only sound is the swishing of the air around the plane, much like the sound I heard after my parachute opened when I skydived. I feel like one of those birds of prey gliding above the ground. I love the sense of freedom from earth soaring sometimes with other birds, but none of them are birds of prey. After a half hour or hour we prepare to land. We circle lower and lower toward the small airport. Arriving back to earth is much gentler than the sudden slamming into the ground I experienced with a parachute landing. We are 1,000 feet off the ground on a straight line to the runway. Unlike a power plane we get only one chance to land. Either it's on the one wheel in front and the one in back of the plane, with one wing dipping to the ground when we come to a stop, or it's a crash landing.

Rarely do these planes crash because they have such a high glide ratios. A glider today has between a 25:1 and 60:1 glide ratio, meaning it will travel say twenty-five feet for each foot it drops in altitude, or sixty feet for every foot it drops in altitude. My J-5 probably had about 18:1 ratio. In comparison, a Boeing 767 has about a 12:1 ratio while the Space Shuttle only had a 4.5:1. So a sailplane, or glider, is pretty safe. This is an amazing experience I recommend to everyone.

Flying a glider or skydiving are very real, but not everything we see and hear is to be believed. Maybe people are willing to ignore reality for the sake of entertainment, which is fine. But it bothers me when entertainment companies take the audience for fools. I'm even more disappointed when the audience is incredibly gullible. Many of the first big "reality shows" grew audiences by having the public vote for contestants. How valid were those votes? Hard to tell, but one has to be a critical thinker, not just accept what is presented for mass consumption.

■ ■ ■

Several years ago I attended a meeting of writers, directors, producers, and other people in the TV and film industry at CBS. Big "Reality" shows were having a major growth across all networks. The speaker that night was a man selected to be an executive for the Reality TV department of a major network. After his presentation, during a short question period, I asked how they maintained the integrity of the votes being made for their show each week. He said, *"Steve, it's all about entertainment. We make sure the people who are most likely to keep the audience watching, remain through the cuts."* This convinced me, it's more a producer decision than an audience voter decision.

Do you think it's a coincidence that these shows say something like, *"America voted,"* or *"You voted,"* but they don't say, *"America decided!"* Probably for good reason, since it's the producers who decide, not the misguided public who think their votes count. Remember, this is entertainment. And everyone in the TV/entertainment business knows that "Reality TV" shows are scripted. I wish people watching some of these scripted "Reality Shows" would just appreciate the entertainment value and not be duped into believing they are real. The real danger is the general public can be easily fooled when it really counts, like in elections!

Reality shows do retakes to get what the director and producers want on screen, whether that is a fake fight, argument, or exciting event to "entertain" the tuned-in public. And what is worse, is this naiveté has spilled over to what people see and hear on the internet or on some so-called "News shows." I want to have more respect for my fellow Americans. I guess "Reality TV" is 21st Century's version of 20th Century "Wrestling TV." I'm still amazed to find people who watched TV wrestling and believed it was real.

Critical thinking takes it on the chin when it comes to the public abortion debate in our country. It "appears" as if there are many people for abortion and many people against abortion, but I don't believe ANYBODY is for abortions. *I wish there would never be another abortion,* but there will always be some medically indicated situations in which such a procedure will be necessary as determined by a woman and her physicians.

A hypocrite can be described as, "someone who doesn't want a certain outcome, and yet will not support a way of preventing that outcome." Isn't it logical that knowledge and instructions on how to safely handle a gun is the best way of preventing accidental shootings? The most effective way to substantially reduce unwanted pregnancies and abortions is by providing birth control and sex education. How can someone who is anti-abortion not support such services and education? It's hard for me to understand why so many people who are most vehemently against a woman's right to decide if she needs to have an abortion, are those who are also most vehemently against sex education and birth control. How do critically thinking humans reconcile these two positions?

When a pregnant woman and her doctor decide the last option possible is terminating a fetus, it's heart-wrenching. This decision doesn't belong to strangers who want to impose their religious beliefs on others. It belongs to that woman, just like which religion, if any, someone chooses to follow, belongs to that person and NOT to a stranger to make this choice for them.

An organization that spends much of its resources educating women, providing information on birth control, and adoption services, is doing whatever it can to help reduce the need for abortions. I think that even if this same organization supports women, who after all their intervention, still make this emotionally difficult choice to terminate "their" pregnancy, have done the right thing for those women.

Our family had four boys when my parents adopted my sister. They first took her in as a foster child at two years old and applied to adopt her almost immediately. Debra had been neglected by her parents, who were drug users and left her with a grandmother. Unfortunately, her grandma was old and not physically able to handle a newborn. Debra was left in a crib all day, for nearly two years. Her grandmother did all she could to care for her.

It was not unusual for Debra, as a teen, to act out, run away, and live on the streets from time to time. But our mother never gave up on her. She kept loving her and bringing her back home. Debra worked hard to help herself. Today she's happily married, was very close to our mother, and while she never wanted to have children, she's a great aunt and terrific role model for her cousins.

I would like to see everyone who actively opposes a woman's right to choose, demonstrate their conviction by adopting a child. Let's make sure there are no orphans and unwanted children, especially for those women who have chosen not to have an abortion and decide to give up that child when it's born. Adoption will make that child's life better, and in the end, our country will have a population of healthier adults.

■ ■ ■

A little boy named Johnny hangs out at the local corner market. The owner doesn't know what Johnny's problem is, but the other boys constantly tease him. They always comment he's two pickles short of a barrel. To prove it, they offer Johnny his choice between a nickel (five cents) and a dime (ten cents) and Johnny always takes the nickel – they say he chooses it because it's bigger.

One day after Johnny grabs the nickel, the store owner takes him aside and says, "Johnny, those boys are making fun of you. They think you don't know the dime is worth more than the nickel even though it's smaller."

Slowly, Johnny turns toward the store owner, away from the other boys. He grins and whispers, "Well, if I took the dime, they'd stop doing it, and so far I've saved nearly $20!"

■ ■ ■

Sherlock Holmes and Doctor Watson are sleeping out in the wild. At 2:00 AM in the morning, Holmes wakes up Watson and asks, "Watson, look up, pray tell me, what do you presume?"

Watson replies, "I see a vast Universe, full of stars and wonder. There is Venus over there, and the Moon is half lit. I know lurking at the center of our galaxy is a black hole with gamma rays occasionally blasting at us. There are billions and billions of planets out there, some of which must harbor life. We are not alone."

Watson would have continued but Holmes abruptly cuts him off, "No, Watson, you idiot! Somebody stole our tent!"

12

HEALTH: LEAST APPRECIATED ASSET UNTIL IT SLIPS AWAY

Good health can make all the difference on your way to the finish line of life. When I was young, I often heard older people say, *"If you have your health, you have everything."* Many of them knew the pain associated with a life failing due to poor health. As youths, we behave as if we are immortal, until we find out we're not.

When we are young, we experience few incidents of young people getting severely ill or dying, unless it's something like a car accident or extraordinary disease. As we age, much more of that is going on all around us, if not among those we know, then we hear from friends about others they know who are seriously ill or have died. Jay, a retired physician, labeled conversations among older people discussing ailments, treatments, and medications, as an "Organ Recital." Sadly Jay died a couple of years after I met him.

■ ■ ■

When we survive a potential life-threatening event, or medical incident, we want to share that experience with friends, so they might learn from our experience, and probably just as importantly, that we benefit from the experiences of others. The first such incident happened to me several years ago. I had flown to L.A. from New York for vacation. Two days after arriving I noticed what felt like a cramp in my left calf. I'm an avid tennis player, not to be confused with being a great player. Such a cramp might have occurred had I been playing tennis, but I was not.

I stayed in L.A. for about a week before flying back to New York, returning to the less than comfortable New York winter I had just escaped. That damn "cramp" persisted, so a couple of days after returning, I called my doctor, Stephen. He graduated from Bologna Medical School, I didn't know him in Bologna, it was only by chance, based on a recommendation from a friend, that we met and I began using him as my doctor. It was a Friday morning; his office was near where I worked in Great Neck, on Long Island, so it was no problem arranging to see him later that afternoon, after work.

I had plans that night with my wife and friends, Ron and Kathy, neighbors in Woodbury, to drive into NYC and have dinner before going to a Broadway show. I skillfully scheduled to see Stephen early enough so my wife could get a ride with our friends and meet me at his office, since from Woodbury, Great Neck is directly on the way to the City. It was going to be perfect timing – we'd still be able to have the evening we had planned several weeks earlier. Curtain time was eight o'clock. They would meet me about five, in time for dinner before the show.

Stephen examines me while we have our usual chat about Bologna – the school, places we went, and things we did around Bologna and Italy – he seems a little perplexed. "Steve," he says, "I want you to see a doctor friend of mine just down the road. He has the right equipment to rule out a blood clot, which is the only thing I'm concerned about. You can be in and out of there in half hour. Have your wife and friends meet you at Dr. Lee's office."

Okay, change of plans. I call my wife with the new address. I'm off to get this test done before they arrive. Dr. Lee is behind black-rimmed glasses and is all business. There is no jovial chit-chat or that warm friendly relationship I have developed with Stephen over the years. It cannot be expected on such a hastily arranged first visit. His receptionist hands me a clipboard with papers to fill out and says, "Dr. Lee is very busy but as a courtesy to your doctor, is fitting you in." I'm thankful and looking forward to making my carefully laid out timetable for dinner and the show.

It's only about twenty minutes before I'm called into the exam room. Dr. Lee arranges my leg in the precise position for two images. "I don't like these last minute appointments, but I'm doing this for Stephen. Back to the waiting room. I'll see you after I review the results of the images." I hesitate but can't help myself, blurting out, "How long do you think it will be?" Dr. Lee clearly restrains himself. "I'm very busy. Be patient... I will not forget about you." I return to the waiting room looking forward to his speedy review, but it's now out of my control.

Ron, Kathy and my wife arrive. I tell them, "Dr. Lee should be out any minute with the results, then we're off to dinner. My wife hands me our two show tickets to put in my pocket. It isn't more than another fifteen minutes before Dr. Lee pokes his head into the lobby. I think he's somewhat surprised to see so many new faces. He motions me into his office, my wife comes with me, we sit in front of his desk. He looks over the images of my leg, leans on his desk with both hands facing me directly. "You must go to the hospital emergency room immediately!" In unison my wife and I say, "What?" This does not go well in calming my wife; it's also a bit jarring for me. It'll just screw up my plans for dinner and the show. This can't be.

He stands up to his full height, about five foot five. "You have DVT, Deep Vein Thrombosis, a blood clot in your leg. You are lucky. If it moved in the last ten days to your lungs or brain, you could have died." I whip out my two show tickets and pitch my case, "We're going to dinner and a show with my friends, the couple you saw in the lobby. Can't I do this when we get back?" I didn't know this at the time, but Dr. Lee has a flair for the dramatic. He strokes his chin, walks from behind his desk around to us, to make sure we can clearly hear what he's is about to say. "Yes, you can go to your show... and dinner, but you may die." Well that will definitely screw up the evening.

It is now clear to me that dinner and the show are not going to happen. Now my dilemma – checking into a hospital to take care of this clot... but

I avoid going to hospitals at almost any cost. They are dangerous places, particularly for people who are not very sick. I once looked up data on hospital-related problems. Each year, in the U.S. alone, due to mistakes by well-meaning doctors and staff, about 450,000 people die. Not just don't get better, not just get sicker, but you heard me... die! That's about 1,250 per DAY! So with little more thought, I ask, "Dr. Lee, is there an alternative to going to the hospital or death?" This question clearly catches both Dr. Lee and my wife by surprise.

Okay, I accept our evening plans are screwed. Now I'm grasping for a Get-Out-of-Hospital-Card, an alternative to getting into our car, driving to Long Island Jewish Hospital as fast as our little wheels can safely travel. Dr. Lee pushes his desk phone toward me. "Call Stephen and ask him." I'm sure he thinks Stephen will agree with his directive. I have nothing to lose, so I call. Stephen is still in his office. "Hey, Stephen, yeah, it's a clot, DVT, and Dr. Lee wants me to go to the hospital... Now... Anything else I can do to avoid both the hospital and death?" Stephen chuckles, then thinks for a moment. "There is one thing you can do." Without knowing what that one thing is, I snap back, "Okay, I'll do it." Now we're making some progress.

"I'll send a prescription to the East Norwich pharmacy as soon as we get off the phone. Pick it up, come over to my house." He gives me directions to his home, which is not far from our home in Woodbury. I'm enthusiastic about avoiding the hospital, but still a little apprehensive about the clot staying put. We tell Ron and Kathy to go on to the show without us. At the pharmacy I pick up a white box measuring about ten inches high, ten inches wide and ten inches deep, and a container of pills. We find Stephen's house on a dark road in East Norwich. I ring the bell, my wife by my side, box and pills in hand.

It's about 6:00 PM, just before dinner in Stephen's house. He meets us at the door, takes the white box from me, leads us into his kitchen, sets the box on the island. His three children, two boys about six and eight, and a girl about four or five, are chasing each other around the house, into and out of the kitchen, making noise as kids tend to do. His wife walks in, introduces herself as she goes about setting their table for the family dinner. I apologize for interrupting their evening over this situation. She brushes it off. "No problem, we're not fancy round here. You won't be in the way."

Stephen picks up the pill container and hands it back to me. "This is Coumadin to break up the clot. Take it every day, but it will take several days before it begins to work." Well that's not very comforting. "Dr. Lee says I'm living on borrowed time, waiting for this clot to take a final hike to my lungs or brain." Stephen opens the top of the white box. "Steve, you ever inject yourself with a hypodermic?" He can see the surprise register on my face. "Are you joking?" I ask. He tilts the box toward me, I see ten hypodermic syringes neatly stacked in the box, filled with drugs ready to inject. "At the hospital you'd be on an IV drip for a few days. You're going to have to inject yourself twice a day for five days." He turns to my wife. "Ronnie, you can do it for him." She goes pale, but gets these words out, "I couldn't even watch without fainting." He turns back to me. "Want to change your mind?" He knows by my expression that's not going to happen; anything but a hospital.

"Show me how to do it." I feel a little harried since we are holding up his dinner and their table is now set. He pulls out the first syringe. It looks like the largest hypodermic needle I have ever seen. Hospitals must have had a hand in deciding how big these should be to discourage people from being "doing-it-yourselfers" like me. "It's simple." How did I know he would start by saying something like that? "How did I get this damn clot?" Matter-of-factly, Stephen says, "Probably happened on your flight to California. It's not uncommon that traveling for long periods of time in cramped quarters, like cars, buses and airplanes. Never cross your legs, walk at least every couple of hours in planes, or stop the car on long drives and walk around a few minutes. If you plan on sleeping more than a couple of hours wear compression socks. Drink lots of water, not alcohol, and eating helps. And finally, periodically move your feet like you're pushing on pedals, up and down, to increase circulation."

Stephen uncovers the business end of the syringe. "Pull up your shirt." He pinches together a good amount of abdominal skin just above my waist. How fortunate I have that pesky extra roll of skin available.

Never thought it would be of any value. It certainly does nothing to give me a trim profile. He sticks the needle into the side of this roll, pushes the plunger until the contents empty into me. I prefer not to watch, but I know it will be my turn tomorrow. If I can't bring myself to do these injections twice a day, I'll end up in the hospital. And that's not going to happen. Stephen tells me, "No exercise or doing anything strenuous until you use up all the needles. We don't want to encourage that clot to move before it dissolves." As we leave the house, the Domino Pizza guy arrives at their door with three pies. Stephen's wife is at the door to receive them. "Told you, it was no bother."

I gave myself the next nine injections, and took the Coumadin for the next six months. The clot dissolved with no further complications. This is now one of those lessons I get to share with friends at "Organ Recitals." I did some research during those five days, and found just how serious DVT is for Americans. About 100,000 people die every year. *About one person every five minutes.* Fortunately, I avoided being part of this statistic with my friend Stephen's help.

But it was not long before I was knocking again on death's door. As much as I stay away from hospitals, when I detect something doesn't feel right, I don't hesitate going to my doctors, to find out what's wrong. Delaying necessary treatments can only let things get worse. Having whatever the hell it is that brings me to my doctor is bad enough, but letting it get worse, is definitely not a plus.

I get on the courts for three sets of tennis, on this beautiful day, at the MountainGate Country Club in L.A. where I play four times a week with a group of about eight to twelve guys. We rotate around and have two or three doubles matches going each time we play. I moved to LA from New York several years before.

I feel great. As usual, my plan is to make no mistakes. Forget it. It never happens and never will. As I get older, getting better is not in the cards. Now I measure success by not getting any worse. If I can achieve this while my buddies, all around my age or older get a little worse, they'll think I'm getting better. But I know the ugly truth.

In the third set, something happens that has never happened before. I play a hard point, almost instantly get out of breath. I stand there for a moment or two. It passes, leaving me feeling just fine. Further into the set I play another hard point, again I'm out of breath. Not being the smartest guy on the court, I finish the set so as not to disappoint my partner and opponents.

However, next morning I call my doctor, Mike B. in Beverly Hills, a good-spirited guy in his early fifties who always greets me with a smile. When I tell him about these unusual shortness of breath events he asks, "Have any other pains, in your arms, chest, or jaw?" "Nope." He says, "I'd like to see you and check you out." I ask, "Sure, when?" Without hesitation, he says, "Now. Come right over, I'll make time for you."

An hour later he runs an electrocardiogram. After looking at the results, he says, "This is not definitive, but if we do a nuclear stress test it will tell me a lot more about what might be wrong." I nod, figuring that sounds right. "Okay, Mike, when?" Again without hesitation, "Now. We'll set it up for you, won't take more than about an hour." By now it's about 10:30. My wife expects me home for lunch, so I still have some time, might as well get it done.

The stress test is indeed stressful – good name for it – because during part of the test I run on a treadmill to raise my heart beats per minute. Mike and the tech monitor my pulse rate, watch my heart activity on the screen. I expect he will tell me to rest up a bit, give me a prescription for some medication, then I'll be off for home. Mike, a very confident and conservative guy, never gets tense or anxious dealing with patients, not even with smart-ass ones like me. So when he says, "Well, there may be a problem, but I'm not exactly sure. You, know me, over-cautious. I called my cardiac friend at Cedars Sinai. He's the head of the department and has agreed to squeeze you in." I ask, "For what?" I'm feeling more like a lab rat these last couple of hours than a guy stopping by before lunch.

Mike smiles his calming, confident look and repeats his cautionary note, "It's just a precaution, but I want you to have an angiogram." Crap, another test and I bet he's not talking about scheduling it sometime in the future. "Let me guess, you want me to do this test this afternoon or tomorrow?" Mike shakes his head, puts his hand on my shoulder and says, "Actually I called ahead. They're expecting you in the next fifteen minutes. Just drive over to Cedars. Go through the emergency entrance to get admitted." His asking me to drive myself over there, a good sign, but going through the emergency entrance seems to negate this warm fuzzy feeling and "take the bloom off that rose." He reassures me, "It's just easier and less complicated to go through the emergency entrance than regular admittance. It'll be fine. You know me, just over-cautious."

I have to call my wife, since getting home for lunch is literally off the table. Now things become more complicated. When she arrives at the emergency room area of the hospital, just before noon, she sees me in one of the exam rooms, attached to every electronic device in sight. It looks like I'm a seriously ill person. I tell her it's just a procedure for patients who enter this part of the hospital. Things are definitely not as bad as it looks. I didn't know what the hell I was talking about.

It is now a little past noon. That head doctor at the hospital has yet to show up to see me. They get me into a hospital room by about 1:00 and tell me he will be in as soon as he has a free moment between patients. At 5:00 he shows up. Saibal is a thin Indian doctor, about forty-five, who has a friendly demeanor like Mike. He has some papers for me to sign and explains them quite simply: "These are required by the hospital for us to do the angiogram." A quick look over the papers and I can't miss the several descriptions of how during this angiogram I can die. "Doc, do I have a choice to sign or not sign?" After a brief hesitation, "I'm afraid not. We rarely have a problem; it's just a precaution to protect the hospital." After such a thorough and comforting explanation, and resounding assurance of, "there rarely is a problem," I sign the papers, leaving my life in Saibal's hands.

Around 7:00 PM the surgical staff comes in my room to take me to the operating room. I'm ready for them to put me to sleep and wake me when it's over. If I don't wake, I'll never know it. I'm thinking the IV they put in my arm before rolling me from my room will take a few minutes before I'll be dreaming about other things. But here I am, watching the ceiling tiles along the hall, all the way into the operating room. Damn, I'm still awake when I see my surgeon, Saibal, dressed for work. "We're going to give you a topical anesthetic and then make a small cut in your right inner thigh to enter your vein which will lead to your heart." I think – "Really, I'm still awake." I want to be out by now, but no such luck.

My surgeon has more to say before they begin. "We're going to see how much of a blockage you have in your heart vessel. If we can use a stent to correct it, we'll take care of it right away, if not we'll have to schedule open heart surgery." Shit… this is now getting serious. Saibal tells me to expect a little pinch. I feel that small cut; the topical only dulls it a little. I'm sure I should be asleep by now. Why am I still awake? Then Saibal tilts a screen above my head so I could see the vessels of my heart. He points out a place where my blood vessel seems to make a right angle. Again my first thought is, why am I still awake? I signed up for this planning on waking up after it was all done. Since I'm still awake I figure I might as well talk to him if he's talking to me. "How was blood getting through that vessel?" He turns to me, "Well Steve, that's the problem. You were hours, days, or weeks away from a major heart attack."

"So, can you fix it now or must I wait to schedule surgery?" Saibal looks over to his operating partner, across my still AWAKE body, and they both nod. "Good news, we can fix it." He now has a discussion with his fellow surgeon as to which size stent to use. After another half hour of them doing their thing, and me having to be AWAKE the whole time, I get back to my room for a good night's sleep. I'm home next day by lunch.

I feel like I just dodged another attempt on my life and managed to avoid arriving at my finish line earlier than I would have wished. I'm so thankful I had good insurance. When the bill arrived, it was all paid by insurance. The total for that one day at the hospital, for the doctors and the procedure to install the stent, was just over $84,000. Having to pay that would have been another attack on my life. How do people survive without insurance? Why do some people want to deny others this life saving protection?

It's been twelve years since I received that stent. All is still going well, and I do all the right things on long flights to prevent DVT.

Michael B, my internist, who I loved as my doctor, decided to become a concierge doctor handling only fifty families per year. He wanted to do so he could spend more time at home with his son who had some serious health condition. My wife and I definitely wanted to stay with Michael B so we asked what his charges are to be one of those fifty families. He said, *"For the first person it's $22,000, then $11,000 for the second person."* Whoa! If we had a third person it would only be another $5,500. But forget about that since there is only the two of us. $33,000 per year was way, way out of our reach. I had to tell him how much we loved having him as our doctor and that we will definitely sign-up when we win the lottery. Daniel took over for Michael B as my internist and my wife, Ronnie, found herself a female doctor. Daniel suggested I use a cardiac doctor in addition to seeing him once a year. He introduced me to a very short, confident, take-charge Indian cardiologist named Sheila in his same suite of offices.

■ ■ ■

The first time I see her she looks down at my medical chart, then at me and asks, "How old are you?" I tell her I'm about two-thirds of a century old. I've never had a birthday since the day I was born, but I have had many anniversaries since the day of my birth. "Oh, just a baby. It's going to be my job to keep you healthy until you're a hundred." Okay, what's not to like about that? Then I find out, to both her and my surprise, her brother is Saibal, who put in my stent. Isn't life just full of surprises and coincidences?

I have always believed I'm responsible, at least to the extent of seeking and evaluating medical care when needed, to help assure my heath. Now that Sheila is on my team, I want her to reach her goal of keeping me healthy until I'm a centenarian. I would be delighted to break the world's record of 122 years old. My blood pressure and cholesterol have been controlled by medication for several years, but since writing this book, and being under her care, I've decided to lose twenty pounds, which may help me get off or reduce some of these meds. I want to help my heart beat for as many years as possible. A loss of twenty pounds will save my heart from pumping blood through about 140 miles of blood vessels (seven miles per pound). To date I've lost ten pounds, seventy miles fewer blood vessels. My heart says, thank you.

This should buy me some extra years. Selfish, I know

Each morning I take inventory of how well I feel, consciously telling myself I'm thankful for my arms, legs, feet and overall body having no pain or discomfort. I'm aware my eyes and ears are also working well. I feel good all over. I do this because I've realized the only time I appreciated feeling good, or not being in pain, was when I was in pain or felt badly. Then and only then would I say to myself, "Wish I felt as good as I did some days or weeks ago, before this injury, illness or physical problem." Even waking up with a bad cold would be enough to make me reminisce about those days when I could breathe without dealing with a runny nose or bad cough. I decided I would rather recognize and enjoy every good day when I'm feeling fine, rather than appreciating them only when I'm not well or hurt.

■ ■ ■

The Pope dies and upon reaching the Pearly Gates to heaven sees a very long line. He walks to the head of the line to enter and St. Peter stops him.

St. Peter: Sorry but you must wait on line, there are no exceptions.
            As he is returning to the end of the line, an old guy in a doctors lab coat and stethoscope around his neck walks past him and St. Peter lets him right in.
            The Pope promptly turns around and steps up to St. Peter.
Pope: I thought you said there were no exceptions. You just let that guy in.
St. Peter: Oh, that was God, sometimes he likes getting dressed up and playing doctor.

■ ■ ■

One day, while strolling down the boardwalk, John bumps into Rob, an old friend from high school. "You look great John," says Rob, "how do you stay looking so young? You must be 60 but don't look a day over 40!"

"I feel like 40 too!" replies John. "That's incredible" exclaims Rob, "How old was your dad when he passed?"

"Did I say he died?" asks John. "He's 85 and is more active than ever. He just joined the neighborhood basketball team!"

"Whoa! How old was your Grandfather when he died?"

"Did I say he died?" asks John. Rob is amazed. "He just had his 104th birthday, plays golf and swims every day! He's getting married this week!"

"Getting married?!" Rob asks. "If he's 104, why on earth does he want to get married?!" John looks at Rob and replies, "Did I say he wanted to?"

13

NEEDS AND WANTS: KNOWING THE DIFFERENCE

Some days I enjoy sitting at an outdoor restaurant on Ventura Boulevard observing people and things around me, cognizant of each effortless breath I take that keeps me alive. I feel the breeze across my face, notice the palette of colors splashed across storefronts, on passing vehicles, and adorned on pedestrians. I know there are many people who can't see colors, many others who can't see at all. For thousands of people, each breath is labored and difficult, so I'm not taking any of this for granted without truly appreciating these gifts I have.

I listen to the noises on the street, the traffic along the road, an occasional "SHUSH" of a bus or truck's brakes, and a horn now and then. Even a bird can be heard periodically, chairs moving around, and the tap of a glass landing on a table by the hand of a waitress. How many people are deaf, never to hear these sounds? I'm not complaining about a single disturbing noise. Hearing them is a gift. I also have never really had a bad day on the tennis courts, or on a golf course, because just being there, win or lose, makes them very good days.

In sports, teammates are the greatest asset. Off the fields and courts there are others who are our teammates as well. They include our co-workers, fellow members of community organizations, clubs, friends and any other groups of people with whom we share a common interest and goal. We all need them in our lives. They make up an important part of our networks. Some are better than others; they're people and people are complicated. I know that every one of them won't meet my every expectation. But I want to believe each person is doing the best they can. Recently the news has made me aware of some people who are extreme deviants from the norm of humanity. These broken people must be isolated, contained and kept from harming others of our species.

I believe in the statement, "Giving is more satisfying than receiving." I think as humans, most of us have a need to give. It's not just about money or things, but can include one's time, offering a helping hand. So whether a wealthy person gives away millions to charity, or a less wealthy person gives their time or a few dollars to help others, they both get the same personal benefit. This fulfills a need to feel worthwhile. By my nature I try to help other people reach their goals and find success. Spending much of my life as a teacher has either fostered this behavior or exemplified it. I'm confident that the success of others does not diminish my own success. I'm perplexed when I see many people reluctant to help others be successful. Seems the accumulation of monetary wealth is a basic driving standard of success for many people seeking happiness. Yet I've seen very poor people who are happy. Therefore it is not just financial wealth.

Ever wonder what's the human fascination with jewelry – sparkly gems and shiny metals? I was curious as well so I did a little research and was surprised to find it began with primitive humans struggling to survive. No, they weren't searching for diamonds and gold. Shiny things in our primitive world were sort because it was often water that created this attraction, without which survival would have been impossible. Here we are today with that instinctual affinity for shiny things, but now it's jewelry and shiny metals instead of water. Financial wealth is a fleeting asset and death the ultimate equalizer. If you survive longer than a millionaire, who has accumulated lots of gems and treasure, you'll be richer than him or her. Nobody, no matter how impoverished, would trade places with a dead millionaire. After death, a millionaire or billionaire can't buy any better an afterlife. It didn't work for dead Pharaohs and it won't work today.

■ ■ ■

I appreciate what I have. Compared to most people in the world I'm wealthy, very wealthy, and it's definitely not all about money. I, like many others, owe a goodly amount of my wealth to the pure luck of my birth. Not only for the family I was born to, but more importantly, where they lived. Being born in America was the first right thing that happened to me, something I truly appreciate. Those born in very poor countries are immediately burdened with often insurmountable barriers to a good quality of life.

Do you have access to safe running water? About 800 million people do not. This includes two million Americans, maybe more, who are unaware of the quality of their water. Is there a toilet and kitchen in your home? About 2.4 billion (this is with a "B") people in our world don't have a bathroom and another 2.7 billion don't have a facility to cook a meal. How about electricity; do you have a plentiful supply? Approximately 1.2 billion people have no electricity. More than a million people are homeless in the U.S., with 25% being children. Many millions of people, maybe billions, don't have a change of clean clothing.

It's estimated that 96% of the world's population don't have cars. And finally, do you need to scavenge around every day for barely enough food to stay alive? Because about *1 billion* people are at the edge of starvation each day. How can I, in good conscience, complain about airline food when most of the people on Earth have never been in an airplane? When I'm eating better each day than more than 95% of the rest of the world, how can I complain about a less than perfect meal? My son, Josh, calls such complaints "first world problems" and wishes everyone in the world only had such problems. But sadly much of the world has real, serious problems, not the trivial ones like which restaurant to eat at, or where to go on the next vacation.

My wealth and that of many others in the Western world includes having freedom, libraries, museums, quality food, clean water, clean air to breathe, a car, and the ability to travel and take a vacation now and then. We all have a bounty of wealth. Based on all these things, there isn't a person I know who isn't wealthy in one way or another. But do they all appreciate what they have? I'm not sure, but I sure do. I also count as my wealth, family, a few good friends and many acquaintances I spend time with most every day. I try not to just look at those who have more, but recognize there are millions, *billions*, of people who have far less. My Dad was emphatic when he told my brothers and me how to behave at buffets. He would say, "Take as much as you want, but eat as much as you take." He often reminded us of many people all over the world who will never have enough to eat.

There is a capitalistic trap that's hard to avoid. The more money most people earn, the more things they buy, the bigger things they buy. From my point of view, too many of us take this beyond what we really need, into the realm of what we are told we want or need. We're inundated by marketing and media trying to convince us of what we must have to be happy. It's an illusion. Warren Buffett is an example of behavior that bucks this American trend of excess. I've read he still lives in the same home he bought over thirty years ago. As his wealth went from millions, to tens of millions, and on to billions, he did not find the need to buy a bigger home. He recognizes what he has, is all he needs.

I believe having a pet is one of the least expensive ways to achieve greater happiness. Pound for pound, caring for any other living thing can make a person happier. Unfortunately, billions of people can't afford to even have a pet. I'm partial to dogs, though I've had fish, hamsters, Guinea pigs, and a bird when I was younger. My dog is affectionate and always greets me with what seems like enthusiastic joy when I come home. Does anyone have a friend, significant other, husband or wife who does the same with the enthusiasm of a dog? Yeah, it may be because I'm his meal ticket, but he doesn't tell me that's why he's so happy to see me. I think cat people feel much the same about their felines. It's hard to get into an argument with your pet, and they are such very good listeners. I've noticed how many people talk to their pets, particularly to dogs and cats. We talk to them a lot, at least I do. In fact, I would venture to say we might express our affection for our little furry friends more than we do to our human mates. I am sure there is room for improvement in this area for most of us.

Getting a pet from a shelter or dog pound is not just saving a life, but the animal, I believe, appreciates us being there for them. I know this may be a little anthropomorphic, but I believe it. Call me a pet romantic!

■ ■ ■

My dog was a chance encounter. One day my wife and I decided to go to Montana Avenue in Santa Monica to walk around and have lunch. Just off Montana, an animal rescue group had several dogs they had recently taken from a "kill shelter" for passerby's to meet and hopefully adopt. A "kill shelter" is a place that takes in abandoned and abused pets and after several days, if they are not adopted, they are killed. Gleason had been on "death row." This rescue group had visited him the day before his scheduled execution and sprung him from certain death.

We see several nice looking dogs on14th Street before going to lunch. Gleason is a bit scraggly. He sits on the lap of one of the people promoting adoptions and looks very mellow. She suggests my wife, "Just take him for a short walk." She does and then we thank them for showing us their dogs and go back to Montana to find a good place for lunch. During lunch we talk a little more about Gleason, then decide to go back to14th Street and take another look, but the people and their dogs are gone.

We call the rescue agency, tell them we thought about it, decided we want to check out Gleason again to consider an adoption. They say, "Sorry, someone else has agreed to take him. If they change their mind we'll let you know." We are disappointed we didn't act more quickly once we decided we wanted another dog after our first one died a few years earlier. The next day they call. "Gleason is available if you still want him. Come down to our offices for an adoption interview, bring a check for $325." Now we think maybe there is something wrong with Gleason if those people decided not to take him or gave him back. We overcome our doubts and pass the qualifying interview. We rename Gleason, Harry. He turns out to be a great dog. We're lucky he's now part of our family. He helps fill our home with more love and someone else to talk to.

There will always be others who have more money, more or bigger things. Businesses promote more is better, newer is better, and bigger is better for the sake of profits. This is their mission to survive. I must admit, I've had fleeting thoughts of what it would be like to live the lifestyle that includes having a very large multi-million dollar home like a few of my friends have here in LA. But I don't think it would make me any happier. Maybe I would be able to take a few more vacations, and the one thing I would be able to do is be more charitable. Most of these friends who have these excesses rarely talk about their drivers, use of private jets and other extravagances. I must admit, it stirs my imagination to fly somewhere in a private jet. But this is clearly a want not a need, one I can't afford. Whether it's more sheep, land, cars, chickens, homes, or money, there will always be those who have more and those who have less. When I went to Delphi, Greece, these words were cut into the stone above the entrance 2500 years ago, "Nothing in Excess." Strange it was in English! No, it wasn't, it was in Greek or Latin, I found the translation in a guide book. A worthwhile saying to live by today!

I'd like a little more money for the security I think it would provide, I am fortunate it is not an obsession. I avoid looking at advertisements in books, magazines or online about expensive homes or other things I can't afford. While some of them may be beautiful to look at, the hidden message is that these are the things I should be seeking for myself to achieve happiness. But it's a false narrative. The work I do is interesting, challenging, often creative and enjoyable, and periodically results in additional income. I often make a list each night, before going to sleep, of the things I can do to improve my chances of success on all fronts, from my writing and any business I'm working on at the time. I try diligently to check off each of them as that next day unfolds. I do my best to achieve success for each and every item and if it doesn't happen, I chalk it up to "not meant to be" and move on.

■ ■ ■

Friend – a word that means different things to many people. For me, not only does it apply to people very close to me, but also to some I see and deal with frequently. While there's a difference between a long-term friend and other friends, I cherish them both. Next to family, friends are one of the most valuable assets I have during my short stay on our planet. There are friends I've lost through distance, time, and others from death. The value of those lost forever unfortunately are not fully appreciated until they are gone. John is a long-time friend I have known for about forty years. We care about each other beyond our working together as co-brokers on commercial real estate.

Lately, I've realized my brother Fred and Ronnie my wife are long–time friends as well. I wonder if many people think of their spouses in this way. They are often the people we've had the most life experiences with over the years. I also count my uncle Bill and aunt Bea in this group since I've known them all my life. Bill, a WWII Vet, is my mother's brother who just turned ninety-four on his way to one hundred. I love talking with him hearing his insightful intelligent take on things based on his experiences. He was always into airplanes like me. He recently told me he was going to change his Living Will. I asked why? "Because I don't want to be unplugged until Trump is in prison!" I vividly remember Bea, my father's sister, who is about ninety-five, taking me, with her husband Eddie, before they had kids, to the Barnum and Bailey Circus and to see Roy Rodgers and Dale Evans' Rodeo Show when I was a little kid. I can't complain about my childhood with such good family around me. I wish everyone had such a benefit, but I know many people have been less fortunate.

As my son matured into manhood, I feel our friendship has been growing beyond that of father and son. I'm pretty fortunate. Friends and acquaintances, all with different personalities, have various traits and characteristics, some of which I admire and others I find a bit abrasive. Interactions with these people, throughout my life, have been critical, complimentary, demanding, encouraging, supportive, compassionate, honest, loving, to name a few. They all help me balance my own behaviors. Those traits I like, I try to emulate, while others I make every effort to avoid.

I have lived in three different States and another country. I had to connect with new people each time, making friends and acquaintances. Now, living in L.A., I've met some terrific people. Many have lived here all their lives, creating close-knit circles of long-time friends. It seems to take more time than in the other places to become part of these long-standing groups, if it happens at all. I sometimes wonder why California, or LA is this way. Maybe it's not the place, but it's me, my age now, versus my past younger me. I was able to get into friend-groups easier when I was younger and those groups I wished to join were also younger.

■ ■ ■

L.A. is the first place I've joined a club, finding members with greatly diverse lifestyles, values and points of view. They can drive cars that range from economical, eco-friendly transportation to $200,000+ performance luxury vehicles. They can be people who fly coach or those who only fly first class or in private jets. This income and net worth schism can also make it a little more difficult to join established groups of friends. I like spending time with friends off the tennis courts as well as across the net. While I wish I could spend more time with all of these friends from the club socially, many of them are "foodies" and knowledgeable wine and liquor lovers. This means they often go to dinner at expensive restaurants. While I have difficulty spending $100 or $150 dollars per person going out for a very special occasion, they often go out for a Friday or Saturday night dinner and regularly spend this amount with other frequent occasions in which they spend $300 to $600 per person. But on occasion they will go to a more moderate restaurant and I can get to spend that extra, off-court time with them socially. A welcome gift whenever it happens. In the past, I would find myself among people almost all of whom were at the same socio-economic level, not by race, but by education and incomes. So this was never an issue.

I often feel connected and thankful for the many people I've met at the club. Some have become pretty good friends on the tennis courts as well having gone out with them and their wives like Toshi, Herb, Mike B, and Mike D, Steve, Neil, Peter, Wally and Al. We appreciate being invited by Hilary to her Halloween parties and Mike D's July 4th party. It's important to me to have the comradery of intelligent decent people and

I've enjoyed the company of them all. As I think about it a little more, I'm so fortunate, because many people in the world probably have fewer good people around them than I do. My quality of life is better because of them. I want to appreciate them, spend more time together when possible while they and I are still here, not because I fear death, but because when it happens there is no going back. I love Toshi's sense of humor. When the topic of dealing with wives came up he said, "When I go to sleep I tell my wife I'm sorry, and when I get up in the morning I tell her again, I'm sorry. This to be sure I cover any mistakes I make when we are awake."

Incredibly, a group of us formed a USTA tennis team at the club and went on to be the 2009 National Senior Champions after winning our matches at Indian Wells for the Sectional Tournament, and the finals in Surprise Arizona. I never would have been part of this terrific accomplishment if I hadn't moved to LA, joined the MountainGate Country Club, and met and played with a group of great guys who were pretty good tennis players.

Many of these friends have generously invested in both of my two short films, knowing they would not make back a single dollar they invested, but believed in me and the life-saving messages in each film. These guys have helped to validate what I do and the quality of my work. I'm particularly thankful for Mike D, Wally, Toshi, and Mike B, who when they found out about my personal health issues, called, texted, or emailed to wish me well and check up on my progress periodically.

Another Mike, let's call him Mike F, works for a division of Warren Buffet's company. He offered to help me reach Mr. Buffet to give him information on a company I thought he might be interested in purchasing. I called Warren Buffet's office, with the contact number Mike F gave me, and spoke to his assistant. She asked about the company, said it sounded like something he would be interested in seeing more information about, and suggested I send it to him for review. I asked for his email. Almost laughing, she said, "Mr. Buffett does not use email, please mail your materials to him." So I sent it to him. Mike F advised me not to hold my breath based on a saying Buffet often cites, *"If your phone isn't ringing, it's probably me not calling."* Well, my phone never rang. I guess he was on the other end, not calling. But Mike F did what he could to help, without asking for anything in return. A good guy.

Jason, who I also call a friend, is a retired seven foot (okay, only 6 foot 11½ inches) professional basketball player, who I invited to play tennis with the group of us every week when he's in town. He hits the ball incredibly hard, and on many occasions holds back a slam to avoid killing me or other players. He doesn't have a mean bone in his entire tall body. I sometimes slip in a moment of frustration and use a colorful expletive, paying homage to my Bronx upbringing. When in earshot of him, I'm embarrassed to show such bad manners. I credit Jason, with his good example on the court when handling momentary frustrations, as part of why I am dedicated to eliminating any further expressed verbal anger, even though it's only directed at myself.

Like others who cared about me, I expressed my wishes to my friend Larry to stop cigar smoking because I saw what happened to my friend Dick. Caring goes both ways. He recently quit, probably because of pressure from his family. I'm sure I was just a tiny voice added to the chorus he came to hear, which will hopefully provide him with both many more tennis matches and life expectancy.

I can't help resenting those who inherited millions of dollars and try to impress others with money they didn't earn, especially if they're not charitable people. This includes both public figures in the news and some of them I have met or done business with over the years. Fortunately I have met very few such people, and those I have met I stay away from the best I can. There's a baseball analogy I've always liked that I feel best describes such people, *"They're born on third base and believe they hit a triple."* In many real estate families in particular, grandfathers and fathers created lots of wealth for their families, then the kids and grandkids of these families go about making a "small fortune" and bragging about what they have done. The truth be told, it's only because they started with a "large fortune." It's a bit of an illusion, or delusion, shrinking the wealth they've inherited. I can't think of a single person I play tennis with, here in LA, who hasn't earned the money they have. It's clear to me they are all very smart, creative hard working people and I'm proud to know them and call them my friends.

I chose to spend much of my life as an educator, a profession definitely not known for wealth accumulation, but it has provided a healthy, happy, and satisfying life for my family and me. Being a teacher has had a profound impact on my life and I hope on the lives of those in my classes. After many years at the front of a classroom, I appreciate the value of helping young people discover and value the truth, and learn to use critical thinking skills for problem solving. I tried to be their guide and cheerleader through their learning process rather than just a simple source of facts. Teaching young people, particularly high school juniors, seniors, and college students has helped me understand younger generations following behind us. It's no small thing when you realize they will be the ones running our country, the world, when we are in our seventies and beyond.

People choose different careers; some provide greater opportunity for accumulating wealth than others. I think most people choose to do things in life based on their passions or innate talents. I once heard someone say, *"If you love what you do, you'll never feel like you have a job."* Some end up in one career or another by chance, accident, circumstance, or through family businesses. Had I chosen a career in finance, or big business management, I would likely have more financial wealth today. I'm a life-long learner, enjoying reading, absorbing as much information on various subjects as possible. Even when I arrived in L.A. I signed up to attend school, this time for screenwriting classes in the continuing education department at UCLA.

The story of my career path was simple; it was almost down to life or death decision. I left medical school in Italy in the spring and took a temporary job as a junior high school substitute science teacher to pay the bills while I was working on my Master degree in Oceanography and Marine Biology. The war in Vietnam was raging on in South East Asia and on TV every night, marches in the streets were building each week. A couple of years after I started, the Draft was initiated by the Selective Service Administration in Washington. While my junior high school students went on to high school, I received a 1A from the Draft meaning they want me to go on to Vietnam as a soldier.

There was a nationwide lottery. There were 366 blue plastic capsules containing birth dates placed in a large glass container and drawn by hand to assign order-of-call numbers to all men within the 18-26 age range specified in Selective Service law. Each day of a year was randomly picked on TV. Those who were the first two hundred numbers drawn were most likely to be drafted. Those picked later could also be drafted depending on how many of those picked were disqualified because of heel bone spurs, or real health issues and other exceptions like being married. One thing commonly done by those with low draft numbers was to enlist in the service of their choice before being drafted into the army. I was number 186, so as they say, "My number was up." About the last thing I wanted to do was to kill Vietnamese people or be killed by them.

The head of the science department, Walter, visits me one day in June, after class, during the last few days of the academic year. "Steve, I heard your birthday is in the lower half of the draw. Have you given any thought about whether you will enlist or just wait to be drafted?" I think for a moment and say, "Neither one seems like a great option." Walter pauses, takes in what I say. "I like the way you teach, I can offer you a full-time science teacher position next year. With your science background you'll only have to take three educational courses to get a teaching degree." I reply rather quickly, "Thanks, but no thanks. Teaching is not what I'm planning to do. I want to get a Ph.D. and then re-apply to medical school here in the U.S."

As he walks to the door to leave, I put some of my things in my bag to go home. He stops and turns, "Not sure you know this, but the government is very keen on keeping as many math and science teachers as possible in our classrooms." I finish packing, "Yeah that makes sense." He leans on the door knob and continues, "They give these teachers a 2S deferment from the draft, for as long as they teach." This is the critical turning point of my life, for the next twenty-five years. One of my highest goals in life now comes into sharp focus, it is not to kill or be killed. I look up, we make eye contact, "You just got yourself a new science teacher."

It was an easy choice; choosing to teach kids all about science, which I love, or carrying a gun through a Vietnam jungle. Thereafter, I taught at the middle school while earning my teaching certification, then later at the high school. While teaching, I completed my Master's Degree at Long

Island University. Soon thereafter I earned my Ph.D. at Columbia and NYU in Biophysics. I was thirty when I re-applied to med school again. I had no doctors in my family, no money to make a substantial donation, and no super high score on the MCAT admissions test, so it was all uphill. Several schools indicated they thought I was too old to be just beginning med school. I didn't get accepted to any school, so becoming an MD was off my career path. I continued to teach, and was appointed by the President of Columbia University as an adjunct faculty member to their International Seminar on Pollution and Water Resources. I wrote a number of research reports, one on the dangers of Asbestos in 1977 that we presented at our annual meeting with the World Bank in DC. A few years later I took a ten year break from teaching to work as a business consultant before returning to teaching until I retired.

My value as a person is not based on comparative financial wealth because my career path did not come with high salaries or big bonuses. It's based on personal accomplishments, the good I've done for others. This is probably true of many occupations of service like nursing, firemen, law enforcement, doctors, and of course teachers. Those who choose businesses are more apt to measure success in terms of financial parameters. Not long ago I received an email from Kirk, a high school biology student I had taught many years ago. He said he decided to become a doctor because of being in my classroom and the love of science and biology I inspired in him. He is now a neurosurgeon, the head of a major research hospital in the Northeast.

I hope there are many more students I have touched who have become positive agents in their careers and are impacting lots of other people they encounter. I am sure this is true of most teachers who are such valuable assets to humanity and our country. It is shocking how little they are recognized in that many struggle to earn a livable wage. While I have less money to show for the many years of teaching compared to other professions, these students are part of my wealth as a person. Of course I can't spend this wealth but I know it's mine. I'm humbled by how fortunate I've been and I constantly try to focus on what I have, not on what I don't have.

It's a struggle in the face of media advertising, and the flaunting of wealth by many of those who have it, whether earned or inherited. The single thing I wish for my son is that he always recognizes a need, as compared to a want, and is able to have all his needs met by what he earns.

Changing our social recognition of success from the things people possess – cars, jewelry, large homes, and big bank accounts – to a better standard of success, may contribute to a more just and happy society. Imagine in the future if the loftiest thing you can achieve is recognition for how much you donate to charities or humanitarian causes in money or time. Studies have shown giving is a powerful way to bring more joy to life for those who give. What if there was a list in every community, State, and nationally, showing in order of those who gave the most in the past year? Being on this list, moving higher from month to month, or year to year, could be the status that matters, while hoarding wealth to increase net worth would become less admirable. The Forbes 500 would then be the list of those who gave the most in a single year. If only this could happen. I'm not sure how the list of the wealthiest people in the country embodies great joy or pleasure to the general population.

Sitting with several friends over lunch one day, after tennis, one of them said, "You got really angry today." I responded, almost as a reflex," No I didn't." When I miss a shot I know I'm capable of hitting, or make one of many mistakes I'm capable of avoiding, I do get very disappointed in my performance and make disparaging remarks, demanding better of myself. This is interpreted by some other players as anger. I totally agree that anger is a negative behavior, one we're better off with less in our lives. This again is part of my motivation to eliminate such outbursts on the court.

Can a person actually get angry at themselves? Anger is defined: "Anger usually develops in response to the *unwanted actions of another person* who is perceived to be disrespectful, demeaning, threatening or neglectful." None of this occurs to me on the tennis court, because everyone who plays with me knows I NEVER get angry at my partner or opponent. So my disappointment in my performance on the court is not about anger.

Nonetheless, I have decided that raising my voice with angry words, even towards myself, will henceforth no longer occur. Thanks Jason.

I describe my decision to change my behavior to my tennis buddies. Then I ask them if there was this one thing that will definitely increase your happiness, will you be able to do it? They all agree they would before hearing what it is I am suggested. Then every one of them says, "No, it's not possible." One of the guys even says, "Yeah, I can do it, but I'd have to be sleeping all day."

I suggest to them, "For an entire day, don't get angry (cursing is an indication of anger) or say anything negative about anything or anyone. If this is too hard, try doing it only until lunch, and if you mess up in the morning start over in the afternoon." Going through an entire day will be amazing. Like recovering alcoholics, it will be a great accomplishment for someone to have many of these days in a row. I'm certain people around us will see a difference. It will be a small step toward becoming a happier, more pleasant person. I'm sure it will help dial down the anger around us as well.

Short of a vow of silence, this is by no means an easy task, as you will find if you give it a try. Go through one day and count how many times you mess up. Of course the challenge, like breaking any bad habits, is to do a little better each day.

I've pretty much eliminated bursts of angry words at myself while playing tennis. It's not because I'm trying to be a better player, at my age, I'm just trying not to get worse. I'm making a concerted effort to reduce these negative outbursts to improve the quality of my life on the court and having this new habit spill into the rest of my life. To be honest, driving on the streets and freeways of L.A. poses an ongoing real challenge for me.

■ ■ ■

Through the pitch-black night, the captain sees a light dead ahead on a collision course with his ship.

He sends a signal: "Change your course ten degrees east."
The light signals back: "Change yours, ten degrees west."
Angry, the captain sends: "I'm a Navy captain! Change your course, sir!"

"I'm a Seaman, 2nd Class," comes the reply. "Change your course, sir."

Now the captain is furious. "I'm a battleship! I'm not changing course!"

There's one last reply from the seaman. "I'm a lighthouse. Your call."

■ ■ ■

Reaching the end of a job interview, the Human Resources Officer asks a young engineer fresh out of the Massachusetts Institute of Technology, "And what starting salary are you looking for?"

The engineer replies, "In the region of $150,000 a year, depending on the benefits package."

The interviewer inquires, "Well, what would you say to a package of five weeks' vacation, 14 paid holidays, full medical and dental, company matching retirement fund to 50% of salary, and a company car leased every two years, say, a red Corvette?"

The engineer sits up straight and says, "Wow! Are you kidding?"

The interviewer replies, "Yeah, but you started it."

■ ■ ■

I'm a telemarketer and I've heard it all when folks want to get me off the call. It's not a job everyone appreciates, but it's a job I enjoy and am proud of.

The other day I called a house and a real nice lady answered the phone, she was really helpful and friendly, she was the type of lady that helps a telemarketer get through a long day.

After some pleasantries I asked if Mr. Smith was in, "I'm sorry", she answered "I'm afraid he doesn't live here anymore."

Now that was a real disappointment being she was a nice lady so I played along, took it all in a stride, "I'm sorry to hear that ma'am. Do you happen to have his new number."

"Sure thing!" The woman cheerfully replied, listing off his new number.

I hung up the phone and quickly called the new number and was surprised to hear a recording. "Thank you for calling Rolling Greens Cemetery…"

14

RELIGION: THE GOOD
AND NOT SO GOOD

I find it admirable that humans, long ago, recognized they were not all-powerful and looked beyond themselves to forces they could not control. They were humbled by nature, and we should still be humbled by its power and awesome presence. Primitive peoples respected the forces of nature, worshipped them. Yet today, with far more science at hand, with supposedly a better educated populace, a large segment of people minimize the reality of large-scale environmental conditions that have the ability to make our planet uninhabitable. Unfortunately, many of these people are decision-makers and influence governmental policies to the detriment of humanity's future.

The "Hope and Faith" organized religions provide is the salve to reduce the burning pain of the miserable existence so many people endure in life. Hope is defined as: "To wish for, but without certainty of fulfillment." Lotteries offer everyone who purchases a ticket, hope they may win. The odds of winning are not important to those who can keep this hope alive until the winning numbers are drawn. For those who have horrendous lives – living in extreme poverty, slavery, with painful diseases, or in war-torn parts of the planet – religion can offer this hope through a deity to save or help them out of this misery. Even if this is a hope and faith in the belief of a mythical afterlife, it helps people get through earthly days. Hope, even based on false beliefs, can bring people faced with terrible situations comfort.

I celebrate religions that create communities of people who share their beliefs, and find the common good in those tenets of a religion *that promote goodwill to all people*. They ask members to volunteer some of their time and resources to benefit those less fortunate. For these reasons, organized religions have a place in modern societies, providing a real value to humanity. If by people believing in an afterlife makes them more apt to be kind and considerate to other people, then it's a good thing.

Organized religion has always been difficult for me to accept as real. I went to Hebrew school in the Bronx to prepare to become a Bar Mitzvah (or be Bar Mitzvahed, as some would say) when I turned thirteen. I was taught to read Hebrew – I was never taught the meaning of what I was reading, but told it was a prayer over the bible (Aliyah) or the selection from the Prophets (the Haftarah) for my particular performance on the date of my ceremony. The Rabbi taught me how to put on Tefillin, two black boxes each containing four passages of Hebrew Scriptures on parchment, connected by leather straps. One box is strapped to my left arm so it rests against my heart – the seat of emotions. The other box is on top of my forehead, over my cerebrum, the seat of intellect. It's supposed to teach us to dedicate ourselves to the service of God in all that we think, feel and do. The philosophical explanation is to remind us not to behave solely by the impulse of our heart, nor to act by reason alone, for that may lead to harsh materialism. While I love the philosophical lesson, this process looks ridiculous and for me is sheer voodoo.

This is a ceremonial ritual for religious Jewish men, after they become a Bar Mitzvah and are praying. It seems as primitive as shaking a rattle to heal the sick, or sprinkling "Holy Water." What's with this Holy Water? It's just regular everyday water, blessed by a priest who makes it holy with prayers, one of them of exorcism. It's supposed to banish demons, heal the sick, send unwarranted grace over a sinner. Give me a break! I think both Tefillin and Holy Water are things men, not women, of organized religions have dumped on their financial supporters, the everyday people who organized religions need to feed their financial coffers and to keep control of during their mortal lives. If today, the Pope or top rabbi said God has told them to stop these practices, everyone attending temples and churches would be just fine with the new rules. Of course this would require everyone to really believe these rabbis and priests actually have a channel to God other people don't have. I don't buy it...

Then there is something called the "Redemption of the Firstborn Son." In the Hebrew bible, the Old Testament, someone wrote that God declares, "Every firstborn among the Israelites, man as well as beast, is mine." God, according to Jewish beliefs, has never asked for child sacrifice, but rather requires the firstborn son to devote his life to the Temple. Imagine if McDonald's made such a declaration to its employees. They would have a great source of future labor. But for a religion, it means more followers and more financial supporters. However, the parents can "redeem" their son by paying 5 silver shekels to a Kohen (a so-called priestly family among the Jews). Here again, there is that elitism within an organized religion, placing some group of people, the priests, senior leaders, and their families, above others. It just makes me uncomfortable. I find it hard to believe this isn't anything but people, over the course of history, behaving badly toward other people for the sake of greed, and to keep or acquire power.

Judaism and other religions seem too full of ceremonial rituals, strange clothing, and accoutrements for both the worshippers in temples and churches, and their rabbis and clergy. It always reminds me of Native Americans doing a rain dance, or other religions making sacrifices of animals to create some desired outcomes. Or praying to make changes in our earthly world, with help from an invisible being who watches over everyone, everything, to make a difference. I think it's just people hoping, like buying a lottery ticket, and hoping to win.

■ ■ ■

With no hocus pocus, and not a mention of exorcism, I can embrace this Apache Blessing:

> May the sun bring you new energy by day;
> May the moon softly restore you by night;
> May the rain wash away your worries;
> May the breeze blow new strength into your being;
> May you walk gently through the world and know its beauty all the days of your life.

As a kid I couldn't believe Santa Claus visits every home in the world in one night, distributes toys to everyone – even if you deduct those 10% who weren't nice. In my own religion we have several levels of religiousness, from the most orthodox to the most liberal. Men wear a tallis around their shoulders, typically white, which has to be rectangular, have four corners and strings (fringes) hanging from the corners. They wear a yarmulke, kippah, or skullcap while in a temple or during services to somehow show respect for God, while others suggest it shows an affiliation with our religion. I'm overwhelmed by just these few things I've mentioned; there are a thousand rules related to the 613 commandments (mitzvoth) in the Old Testament that religious people believe are important for their ticket to heaven. Another concept that boggles my mind.

Based on all this, I try to imagine the birth of the earliest organized religion among cavemen, many thousands of years ago. There were probably guys with names like "Og" and "Bo" – not likely they had last names back then. Imagine listening in on these two guys after a hunt, as they sit by their fire (yes, control of fire has already been discovered). They've reached a ripe old age of twenty something. They're bloodied, in pain, exhausted, having lost two other hunting buddies killed by savage beasts earlier in the day. This conversation could not have happened earlier than about 100,000 years ago, when scientists believe language first developed. It amazes me that today on planet Earth there are 5,000 languages.

Bo, a hairy, smelly brute of a guy, turns to Og, also hairy and smelly. The conversation might have gone something like this;

"Og, hey this sucks. It's damn hard and tiring going out on these hunts, it's dangerous as hell; we can get killed." (Of course this is just a paraphrase as cave-talk was less descriptive then.)

Og, not the most intelligent expression on his face, stirs the fire with a stick, leans back and uses every mental nerve cell at his disposal in his still evolving brain. He looks at Bo while chewing on dinosaur meat, "Yeah, it sucks." (*Just joking*, unlike what some religions say, dinosaurs and humans never lived at the same time. Dinosaurs went extinct millions of years before humans appeared on Earth).

Bo being the smarter of the two, gets an idea that will change the human world forever. He says, (remember this is in early caveman talk) "What's so frightening that every one of our cave-mates would be soiling their animal skins?" Og, not the sharpest guy in the tribe, replies, "It will stay dark forever." Bo nods in agreement, but it wasn't where he wanted to go. Bo presses on, "What else would have them curled in a knot?" Og, stirs the fire a little more, his eyes brighten, he's got the answer, "Animals we hunt all disappear!" Another good one, but by now, Bo has run out of patience. "The heat leaves our body, no talk, no eating, we start to smell. We die," says Bo, "...and never walk around again!"

Og agrees, "This would be very bad." Bo poses another question, "What if we get paid to guarantee a better life for everyone who dies?" Og's brow furrows as the one wheel in his mind turns. (This is before multiple wheels evolved in our brains.)

"Where do they go?" says Og. Bo is laying out a concept here and is not going for specifics. "Who cares! Away, into the clouds, on top of mountains, across the waters, doesn't matter?" Og points out, "But we don't know how to do that." What has not gone unnoticed by Bo is that those who have died never return. Bo beams, "Yes, but nobody ever comes back to tell on us."

Upon returning to their cave they tell their cave-mates a tale of seeing the spirit side – death – and having been given special powers. They are now messengers, later to be dubbed priests, rabbis, holy men, to let everyone know the rules and rituals to follow for a wonderful, guaranteed afterlife, so much better than on Earth. Bo tells their cave-mates, while Og nods his head, "To do this special service for all of you, Og and I must not be distracted by having to hunt, skin animals, or do other chores around the cave. We must focus our time communicating with the afterlife and the spirit world." From that day on, others in the tribe had to care for the holy men by providing food, shelter, and protection so they can continue to provide this "valuable," unconfirmed, uncontested, guaranteed service.

It's not long before the first cave dweller drops dead, an old women of at least thirty-five. Bo and Og are put to the test. They must guarantee this old cave women's clan a great afterlife for her. Bo dresses Og up with feathers, furs, face paint and finds a special animal bone for Og to hold. He plans with Og that after each of Bo's chants, Og must touch the dead lady with his special bone. Bo chants various noises, periodically looks to Og for his stick touch. It's a lengthy ceremony, maybe 15 minutes, none of the cave-dwellers had much of an attention span. After they are done, Bo assures everyone attending the service that the deceased is now off to a wonderful afterlife, leaving her used up body behind. So here we have the first insurance plan on Earth. Brilliant!

Thereafter, religions become the longest lasting companies in the world. They provided AFTERLIFE Insurance while insurance companies to follow will provide mortgage, auto, life, funeral and other insurances. These companies (organized religions) required their Afterlife insured to attend meetings (usually on weekend) and to even bring their children to these meetings so they too will be insured for the rest of their lives by providing funds (donations) to the companies (organized religions) to build and expand their businesses. Some religions even stipulate it must be 10% of income. Actual insurance companies charge a premium each year you're alive. There's no comparison – in one case the insurance company pays the family a large sum of money to help make up for their loved one's absence, while the church, synagogue, or mosque gives the person who died a ticket to heaven to cash in for a good Afterlife. No surviving family member gets a check from the organized religion. Nobody will ever know if the dead person got his/her money's worth, because it was all based on faith, no proof, and no evidence and "…nobody comes back to tell on them." Good business, right! It's a perfect non-refundable purchase.

Shortly after attending my Bar Mitzvah, my grandfather Harry, a tailor, died. I loved spending time with Harry. He never spoke to me like I was a kid. He bought me my first two-wheeler bicycle, I learned to ride it on the Coney Island Boardwalk near his home in Brighton Beach, Brooklyn. From the time I was eight, until he died, I would go into Manhattan with him a couple of times a year. We would always have lunch at the Horn & Hardart Automat restaurant which had inexpensive food in little compartments that required coins for payment. There was a machine Grandpa Harry would put a dollar into and out would come twenty nickels. Once you inserted the correct number of nickels into the slot by the little window compartment showing the food you wanted, the front door opened so you could take out your food. My favorite chocolate cupcake cost three nickels. I'd get one for dessert each time we went.

We would talk about everything going on in the world. If it were true that dead people get to see those who have died before them, he would be one of those people I would like to see again, to talk about all the things that have happened since he died. I would love to see my brothers and parents as well, but I know this is a fantasy. Maybe those who really believe this fantasy are happier knowing when they die they will get together with lost friends and loved ones. It doesn't matter if it's true or not, because once the believer dies, they will never come back to tell anyone anything. They're dead!

And where is heaven? Have any of you ever heard your commercial pilot say, "Look out your windows, we are passing through Heaven on our way to cruising altitude at 35,000 feet. You may get to see a relative or someone famous." No... We never hear this from our pilots. There's nowhere heaven can be... but in the minds of the living.

■ ■ ■

Maybe my perception of organized religion, including my disbelief in an afterlife, is too cynical. So I decided to do a little research into how it all began. Reluctantly, I was prepared to find out my story about Bo and Og might not be exceedingly accurate. At least I had hoped so when I began my search. My investigation into the three major religions is abbreviated, as there is so much history that can be told, but I think I hit the highlights that provided me both with admiration and in some instances, disappointment. Here then is my brief education about the genesis of these religions. I used several primary informational sources from the three religions to get a clearer picture of origins and practices.

The beginning of organized modern religions seems to have begun earlier than 2000 BC, pre-dating Judaism, with the Iranian prophet Zoroaster. Zoroastrianism entered recorded history only about 600 BC; it was the state religion of pre-Islamic Iranian empires until about the year 650 AD. Zoroaster pays tribute to a deity of wisdom, Ahura Mazda (Wise Lord) as the Supreme Being. His teachings influenced Judaism, Christianity and Islam. There are still about 2.5 million followers of Zoroastrianism in Iran and India. Its basic maxims, include:

- Good Thoughts, Good Words, Good Deeds
- There is only one path and that is the path of Truth.
- Do the right thing because it is the right thing to do, and then all beneficial rewards will come to you.
- There is only one God, the singularly creative and sustaining force of the Universe.

Zoroaster states that human beings are given a right of choice, because of cause and effect, and are also responsible for the consequences of their choices. After reading this, I'm in, except for there being a God. Can you imagine if all people would follow these maxims, the kind of world we would have?

Based on what I see in the world, these first three maxims make so much sense. I find the fourth maxim impossible to be true. An all-powerful God would not allow so many people to suffer from wars, epidemic diseases, and other natural disasters. *Zoroaster's teachings focus on responsibility.* Whoa! This sounds so right. Based on recorded history, from what I see today, I wonder where and how organized religions have gone so wrong. I decided to take a look into the main foundations of organized religions – their Bibles.

■ ■ ■

To my surprise, the first thing that comes to my attention is there were thirty authors of the Old Testament. They started writing it during the 1300s to 1200s BC; it was finished in the 500s to 400s BC. The New Testament had ten authors who began writing it fifty to one hundred years after Jesus died, finishing about 150 to 200 AD. The Quran had no known authors – it was written over twenty-three years in the 6th Century. All these facts make great trivia questions.

The Old Testament is divided into three parts: 1) the Law, 2) the Prophets, 3) the Psalms and Proverbs. Moses wrote the first five books of the Old Testament (the Law), called **the Torah**. These original scrolls were given to the priests of the temple (like rabbis) so they could be placed in special sleeves attached to the side of the "Ark of the Covenant." Now this makes finding this Ark more meaningful to me. Priests, descendants of Aaron, Samuel, Jeremiah and Ezekiel, wrote the other books. Other non-priest authors included David who is considered the main human author of the Psalms, though others contributed, including King Solomon. David's son is credited with providing much of the Bible's wisdom. Many prophets also contributed to the Old Testament. There were twenty-two books written, one for each letter of the Hebrew Alphabet.

There seems to be much more information about the writing of the New Testament than the Old Testament. Maybe it's because in Judaism there are only various levels of orthodoxy while in Christianity there are more diverse sects of the religion. My initial research uncovered a goodly number of scholars who believe many books of the New Testament were written by people claiming to be Peter, Paul or James and who were, in fact, none of them. Not wanting to denigrate their cherished texts by calling many of the books forgeries, theological scholars chose to use another term for such books, "pseudepigrapha."

I found a consensus among many Christian scholars, other than fundamentalists, that the book "2 Peter" was not written by Peter; seven of the thirteen letters credited to Paul are his writings, while six of these thirteen are not; and the book "1 Timothy" attributed to Paul, was written after his death by someone else. This is significant because "1 Timothy" addresses an author-created issue that women were speaking out and were teaching men. The person who wrote this tells women to be silent and submissive. This branded Paul, who was not the author, as a misogynist. Many church leaders have subsequently used these writings to oppress and silence women.

During my research I came across another rule for Catholic priests that has always baffled me. Why have priests been required to practice celibacy? These priests are expected to offer guidance and help their parishioners regarding dating, relationships, and marriage. Does this make any sense? I followed the history of this element of Catholicism from its origin to today and found it interesting, disappointing, as well as incredibly dishonest.

In the First Century, Peter, the first Pope, and Jesus' chosen Apostles were mostly married. Clearly celibacy was not Jesus' idea. In 385 AD, when Pope Siricius left his wife (or maybe she left him), he decreed priests could no longer sleep with their wives. As far as we know, his wife might have thrown him out when he decided to take the Pope job. Then a really rabid misogynist, St. Augustine, wrote in 401, *"Nothing is so powerful in drawing the spirit of a man downward as the caresses of a woman."* I think this guy had serious interpersonal issues. Initially I thought he might have been gay, but surely, even a gay man would not have such a repulsion toward women. He had stature in the church, so what he said apparently mattered.

I continued my research to find in 567, the 2nd Council of Tours, declares any cleric found in bed with his wife would be excommunicated for a year. Again we have people, not the original prophets, making rules for church employees that will impact millions of followers into the future. Then in 580, greed raises its ugly head when Pope Pelagius II decides not to bother married priests so long as they don't hand over their property, or other assets to wives and children upon their deaths; it must all go to the church.

Fast forward almost 500 years to 1074 when Pope Gregory VII says, *"Anyone to be ordained must first pledge celibacy to escape from the clutches of wives."* What were his interpersonal issues? This would attach itself to the Catholic Church for hundreds of years to follow. Finally, in 1095, in the least loving, uncompassionate action, contrary to the loving teachings of the religion's prophet, Pope Urban had priests' wives sold into slavery and their children abandoned. Quite a proud history!

If made up, all this would be hard to believe. Troubled and damaged people – Popes, religious priests, writers – have taken this religion far from the teachings of their original prophet, Jesus. I find this sad, because at its beginning there was hope for this religion to stand up to the tyranny of the Roman Empire and those who controlled Judaic temples, to show the world a better way, with more compassion, love, and concern to all, and particularly for the less fortunate.

We now have some idea of who wrote some, or all, of the Old and New Testaments. So who wrote the Quran? It was not Mohammed. He was illiterate, unable to read or write. The key message in the Quran is to believe in one God, stay away from sin, lead a devoted life earning God's pleasure. Life after death gave glad tidings for those who obey God, but warned of punishment in hell for those who choose to disobey him.

The Quran was written in Arabic; no one has ever taken credit as the author, or even as a contributing author. It's thought the Quran was compiled under the supervision of Mohammed or written after his death by Iman Ali. Still others believe it was compiled after the Prophet's death by someone other than Ali. It's a real tribute to Mohammed that what he preached as an Arab was so contrary to the Arab way of life at his time. Arab culture treated women as animals, while he said they should be equals. Gambling was rampant at the time, yet he said it was wrong. He said charging someone interest on a loan was not right, yet it was customary in the Arab business world to levy high interest charges. He was against drinking alcohol, yet it was common among the Arab population. It was bold and courageous for him to stand up to these business-as-usual behaviors among his fellow Arabs, at a particularly intolerant time.

The births of these major religions have interesting origins. Now I have a better understanding how organized religions seemed to have veered off course – not because of the prophets who set the values of these religions, but because of those people who made their own rules, building these religions into businesses through greed and the intoxication of power.

■ ■ ■

When I compare the balance of good done by organized religions versus the damage, hate, and death promoted by religious dogma, the historical balance sheet sadly favors the latter. Many organized religions provide humanitarian programs that offset this otherwise awful report card. But the wars and violence they've caused in the name of these religions, prejudices they've promoted, and inequalities fostered between men and women, are almost immeasurable. The killing between religions continues to today.

The shackles organized religions have burdened people with have often been overbearing, minimizing human pleasures, often denying millions of people their inalienable rights of life, liberty and the pursuit of happiness. This should not just be an American standard, but should be the standard for all humanity. Being good neighbors, whether of the same or different faiths, should not be a difficult task, yet religions have often set themselves against one another for the sake of building up their own organizations at the cost of others. This has become big business; otherwise each would be happy to do as much good as they can in the spirit of cooperation, not in violent competition.

I wonder what the reaction of Moses, Jesus and Mohammed would be if they visited our planet today. Would they find the people running their synagogues, churches and mosques all honorable, ethical and moral? What would they think of TV evangelists, politicians, all those professing to be good Jews, Christians, Catholics, or Muslims?

When religions distort or ignore scientific facts to foster their own realities I find it deplorable. It's amazing to me that less than half of all Americans believe in evolution? There are museums and libraries filled with evidence, including fossils, proving there has been life on Earth for billions of years. How can anybody believe it only began 6,000 years ago? This is an ignorance promoted by organized religion, a great disservice to humanity.

It had long been thought Earth was the center of our solar system, if not the entire universe. Copernicus, a fellow alumnus of my school, attended the University of Bologna 466 years before me. Thirty years after he graduated, in 1532, he determined the sun was at the center of our solar system and it was the Earth that revolved around the sun. So how is it possible today, about one in four Americans, almost 500 years later, still believe the sun revolves around the Earth? *Does this bother anybody but me?*

Have we put so little effort into educating our citizens that we have crippled their ability to make good educated decisions about anything important – climate change, air and water quality, preventing extinction of species, etc.? This ignorance does not entirely lie at the doorsteps of organized religions. It seems politics has also been guilty of promoting false science to serve its short-term gains. The Vatican Observatory has been at the forefront of astronomical scientific research since 1774. Shouldn't organized religions educate the masses to become more knowledgeable than the primitives who had little or no science to help them understand the world around them? Or is ignorance a tool to help control followers whether it be by religious leaders, corporate executives, or politicians?

When organized religions promote "Faith," are they really selling insurance? Faith is powerful. It's defined as: *"Belief, trust and loyalty to a person or thing; or unquestioning belief that does not require proof or evidence."* No need to look any further than TV evangelists to see the extensive depth of greed they exhibit as they prey on the poor and ill-educated, separating them from their money, in exchange for the guarantee of a much better afterlife. Not unlike what I speculated Og and Bo did with their cave mates. A dictator wants all his people to have hope, wishing and expecting something from him without the certainty of fulfillment. Cults and organized religions depend on followers having faith, unquestioning belief, without proof or evidence, and this goes for whatever the people running a religion say is true. This has become more evident as a tool used by politicians to garner votes based on lies and misinformation.

In the past, priests, rabbis, and religions had to keep upping the ritual show, so they took it to a bloody place. Animal and human sacrifices were routinely performed, promising desirable outcomes like rain, successful hunts, victories over enemies, or good crops; hardly an effective way to control nature, but they didn't know any better. For humans, I've found perception is reality, so if it rained after sacrificing a virgin, the priests took credit. If it didn't rain, they could blame it on the impurity of the dead virgin. Who was to question them? I can't help thinking about how primitive humans went about choosing who to sacrifice. Did they pick the girl who wouldn't give them a second look in fire-making class, or the daughter of the guy who called them names in school and took away their toy stick?

Organized religions initially collected goods and services to support their special people called "Priests" or "Holy Men," those proclaiming a unique relationship with the afterlife through spirits and Gods. Later, money became the currency to buy good fortune on Earth and better afterlives. I read that seventy-five percent of Americans today believe in a deity. I'm guessing most of these faithful religious people also believe, without any proof, there is a better afterlife waiting for them if they follow the rules and the rituals required by those who run their religions. Can someone believe in a God and not in an afterlife?

I believe the outcomes of team competitions depend on skills, training, cooperation among teammates. How does religious belief possibly carry over to sports? I find it a bit disingenuous when players on opposing teams ask for help, or give thanks for divine assistance to win a game. Does each team have a different God, one more powerful than the other, like primitive humans who had many Gods thousands of years ago? Or are they asking this same one God to favor them over their opponents? Why should she? Does this make any sense?

People are told to believe their God is all powerful, indoctrinated to have faith this is true. Faith being: ... *unquestioning belief that does not require proof or evidence.* When there's a disaster like a hurricane, tornado, or flood, it baffles me why an all-powerful God has no responsibility for the death and damage. However, people are quick to gush over the kindness and generosity of that God they thank for any who have survived the catastrophic death toll of the event. The news will interview survivors who will say, "Thank God. It's a miracle, we prayed and were saved as was that little child we just found in the rubble." This when scores of others have been killed, who also prayed.

■ ■ ■

When football, baseball or any other sports teams win, the manager is praised. When that team messes up, loses a big lead, or loses the game, the manager is blamed. Shouldn't an all-powerful deity be held to this same standard? When good things happen, like needed rain, the deity should be praised. But when deaths of innocent people occur, in natural disasters or wars, shouldn't the deity be held responsible?

Have we risen even a tiny step above those primitive humans who worshipped Sun Gods? Did disasters and wars give rise to the invention of the devil? If so, then God is not all powerful. If he was, none of these bad things would happen. Even if there is no God, and no afterlife, religion may be a little like the placebo effect, in that whether it is true or not, if it brings peace and pleasure, while not hurting other people who believe differently, I think it's okay. Unfortunately, belief in different Gods has often had the opposite affect among radical believers.

I'm still convinced the major insurance companies on Earth are not the commercial entities that charge premiums. I think they are organized religions procuring money and support for their multibillion-dollar organizations. They assure their members they will earn a good afterlife if they are true believers, follow their organized religions' rules and customs, and most importantly financially to support their religious organization's opulent existence.

■ ■ ■

Catholicism may yet find its way back to its hopeful, loving, and uplifting roots, all of which are very much needed in the world today. I have found a voice beginning to flush out some of the misdirected dogmas. Pope Francis has verbalized that Adam & Eve is a fable, not real. He has now made a correction in the church's long-held belief of the past, which was a dramatic departure from real science.

But more importantly, in his latest revelations, Pope Francis said:

> *"Through humility, soul searching, prayerful contemplation, we have gained a new understanding of certain dogmas. The church no longer*

believes in a literal hell where people suffer. This doctrine is incompat-
ible with the infinite love of God. God is not a judge, but a friend and
a lover of humanity. God seeks not to condemn, but only to embrace."

I admire him for taking this stand in light of many in his church who
have strongly held beliefs contrary to his. The Pope is taking a stand, like
Mohammed did contrary to his Arab culture in his time. Pope Francis is
speaking in behalf of compassion, what is right, and against what is wrong.

Pope Francis gave a speech recently in which he declared:

"All religions are true, because they are true in the hearts of all those
who believe in them. What other kind of truth is there? In the past,
the church has been harsh on those it deemed morally wrong or sinful.
Today, we no longer judge. Like a loving father, we never condemn our
children. Our church is big enough for heterosexuals and homosexu-
als, for the pro-life and the pro-choice! For conservatives and liberals,
even communists are welcome and have joined us. We all love and
worship the same God."

In this revelation and speech he has, at least in words, vanquished much
non-science, took a giant stride to remove hate or intolerance toward those
who are different, and pushed aside competition between the religions,
joining them together for all people who have faith in a God, he identifies
as one and the same for all. While my beliefs have not changed, I understand these organized religions better than I ever have before.

■ ■ ■

A new monk arrives at the monastery, is assigned to help other monks
in copying old texts by hand. He notices they are copying copies, not the
original books.

The new monk goes to the head monk, points out that if there was
an error in the first copy, that error would be continued in all the copies
to follow.

The head monk says, "We have been copying from the copies for centuries, but you make a good point, my son." So, he goes down into the cellar with one of the copies to check it against the original.

Hours later, nobody has seen him. One of the monks goes downstairs to look for him. He hears sobbing coming from the back of the cellar, finds the old monk leaning over one of the original books crying. He asks what's wrong.

"The word is celebrate!" says the old monk.

■ ■ ■

A priest and a pastor are standing by the side of a road holding up a sign that reads "The end is near! Turn around now before it's too late!"

A passing driver yells, "You guys are nuts!" He speeds past them.

From around the curve, they hear screeching tires – then a big splash.

The priest turns to the pastor and says, "Do you think we should just put up a sign that says, 'Bridge Out' instead?"

15

GROWING OLD: NOT AS EASY AS IT LOOKS.

I remember this great saying, but not who said it, *"A longer life is a privilege, not afforded to everyone."* I think a healthy life is indeed something to be appreciated. I put this on my stationery and emails: **"Treat Each Healthy Day as a Gift."** Each morning I take a quick inventory of my health, saying to myself, "I am happy and fortunate I feel so good today."

Nature becomes a little crueler to us as we age. Primitive women, in general, became less attractive to men after menopause because nature did not want men to waste their sexual time with those who no longer could bear children. Older men escape this fate for some number of additional years, but not forever. Men retain their ability to produce viable sperm into their more senior years, and have traditionally been able to provide security to younger females. But this too doesn't last too long. Many women today don't need or want the security modern males can provide. While older men will still find young women exceedingly attractive, it's unlikely to be reciprocated on an instinctually physical basis. However, in modern society, wealth not brawn provides security and safety, unlike in the distant past. This alone will draw some women to older men.

The years before now have felt like they sped by in a flash. After aging past two-thirds of a century, the days and weeks now feel longer, or at least feel like they are moving more slowly. Maybe because I no longer have a set daily and weekly routine and must decide how to fill each hour and each day. I'm living more in the now than ever before. Less looking toward the future, as I did when I was younger, when I paid too little attention to each day. It was well after fifty that I began my life as a film writer and producer, so the Fall of our lives can be a beginning for many new things – not just the end of experiences begun long ago.

One of the most important things I've learned over these years, and there are many, is the way we perceive others is through the lens of how we see ourselves. If we are often angry, we are quick to see anger in others. If we are considerate and open to new ideas and opinions, we see the kindness and authenticity in others. If we are unreasonably demanding and intolerant, we find others mean and rigid.

Before I bathe in my privilege of life, I want to explore for a moment, the darker side of growing older. Who decides how long you or I must live, if we decide to end our life? For some people, the last weeks, months, or years of life may be a long series of uncomfortable, painful, or even torturous days and nights. We should have the choice to end such a life if it's unbearable to remain alive. Euthanasia somehow has violated the professed righteousness of some organized religions or politicians, who have used every means possible to deny people the right to end their own lives and relieve themselves of extreme pain. Euthanasia comes from the Greek words, Eu (good) and Thanatos (death), thus meaning "Good Death, Gentle and Easy Death." Since each of our lives are generous gifts from our parents, and belong to us first and foremost, why should others have any say over this gift?

Many people who choose to end their life do it in conjunction with their doctor's consultation, while they are of sound mind, having considered all alternatives. It's usually far less violent than those who choose suicide by their own hand. The person who chooses to end their life in this way does not put a financial burden on public health services; quite the contrary. They probably save the public medical system hundreds of thousands of dollars, to say nothing of the cost to their family having to watch them suffer, unable to end their pain.

If those people who choose to follow the rules of their religion decide not to take their own lives in this manner, then so be it, because it should be their choice. The exercise of power over the choices of others, by strangers or the government, is unacceptable. If I belong to a club that does not permit drinking, would it be right to prohibit others outside the club from drinking? This would be absurd. It only takes a brief reminder of prohibition. If I received a car as a gift from my parents, should anyone other than me decide when to sell it, give it away or junk it? Each of our lives are ours only. It would be a travesty if someone during temporary depression made an irreversible choice, but when it comes to euthanasia, this is not the case.

■ ■ ■

Once you pass the proverbial hump in life, around fifty-plus years, and you've been living with someone for a long time, there's an inescapable thought that occurs now and then, at least it does for me. When my wife doesn't show up when expected, especially at night, the human mind, or at least mine, tends to think the worst. What if she was in an accident, or just had a heart attack and died? I don't know how hard it would hit me, but I think it will be harder on my son. As a young adult he hasn't given death much thought during most of his young life, while those of us much older have lost people around us. I think the death of someone close shakes a young person's sense of immortality, because they rarely if ever consider their own death. Why should they?

If my wife suddenly died, it would cause a host of uncontrollable thoughts and questions to flash through my mind, some logical and others absurd. Firstly, a most serious issue – I would have to walk our dog all three times a day. How do I handle the funeral? Do I have one? Too much celebration, people will think I'm happy she's gone; too little, many will think I didn't love her enough. What do I do with vacations already booked? Cancel at great expense, go alone, or take someone else? Who? I draw a blank. I'd have to cancel because I would be thinking about her each day I was away. Crazy questions would surely keep popping into and out of my mind as this life-changing event would explode my way of life.

How will I handle her death? Will I be able to reconcile it as being the natural process of life and continue doing the things I do, day to day? Or will I need to take some time off to appreciate how my life will now be changed forever?

And then, she walks in the door. This will happen again and again depending on how late she returns home. It may really happen one day, it could be either her or me not coming home for that last time. Am I the only one who thinks such thoughts? I think not. What would I expect if it was me, and she had to deal with all these questions and issues? I won't care, because I'll be dead, but I will let her know my wishes before my death. It's the best I can do to be helpful after I'm gone.

When I was much younger I never thought about my own mortality. But I think it smacks us all in the face when someone dies who is at or near our age. It sends a reality spike through my system when I read about a celebrity who dies of natural causes, or some illness, who is either younger or a few years older than me. This drives me to re-dedicate myself to living the most I can every day. This was especially true when I have faced potential death numerous times in the past. Each time I jumped from the open door of a Cessna 150 airplane, from 3,500 feet, with just a flimsy parachute on my back, I cherished living even more.

■ ■ ■

I recall also having thoughts of my own demise when I was working in Brussels during one trip, many years ago, before my son was born. I traveled to Belgium about one week per month for a few months while consulting for the Goemans Group.

Because of my contacts with an Israeli body armor company, Jean Claude Goemans arranges a meeting for us to make a presentation to the Turkish Ambassador in Brussels. The Israeli company provides me with two sample Kevlar bulletproof vests, one just plain white, worn under clothing; the other looks like a blue suit vest worn under a sports or suit jacket. This was not my primary consulting role for the Goemans Group. They dealt more with financing ore processing plants in French-speaking

Africa. But we did get involved with the building of an airport in Kuala Lumpur, Malaysia, and some business with the Thai government regarding U.S. military aircraft.

This vest deal seems pretty straightforward until the last minute before the Turkish car pulls up to the Amigo Hotel to pick us up. I always stay at the Amigo as a guest of Jean Claude's. When not at his home on the North Sea, he uses the top-floor suite as his Brussels offices for business in town. Centrally located, a block from the Grand Place in Brussels, it has great old world charm. The hotel lobby floor is made of street stones from around 600 and the building has been there since the early 1500s. Jean Claude walks with me to the front of the hotel to wait for the car.

We see the car approach when he turns to me to say, "I must attend another meeting in a few minutes that can't be rescheduled, you must handle this one alone. The Ambassador is a good friend, I'll call him before you arrive. Personally express my regrets." I often handled important meetings on his behalf, but usually not on such short notice. My plan is to present the two options to the Ambassador and discuss the basic terms of the sale of bulletproof vests for the security personnel at all Turkish Embassies around the world. This seems pretty basic and straightforward. What can go wrong?

Their shiny, clean, black car, the kind you would see following a funeral hearse, pulls up. A large guy gets out of the passenger side, opens the door for me to get into the back seat.

When we arrive at the embassy, another large Turkish guy steps to the car, opens my door and leads me through the front door of the embassy. I carry a black garment bag with my two samples and a briefcase. Again, two really big guys with mustaches approach. I'm getting the impression I'm meeting the entire Turkish football team one full-back at a time. One of them takes my garment bag and briefcase, and searches them thoroughly looking for who knows what. The other guy checks me all over. He's not looking for candy or other hidden snacks.

His jacket flaps open, I see a gun strapped under his arm. Were they expecting an assassin? If so, this is definitely not a place I want to be visiting today. He takes my wallet, checks my ID, then hands it back. So far not a word is spoken until his deep authoritative voice booms, "This way." They lead me to a small elevator that can barely fit the three of us. I'm feeling like they have maneuvered me into a hole in the middle of the elevator as they both tower over me.

The door opens to a well-furnished living room with warm upholstered furniture, drapes, and several colorful rugs. The two security men remain as guards by the elevator. The Ambassador walks in. A well-groomed, mustached man, he is also of large stature wearing an expensive suit. "Dr. Hartman, please have a seat." He sits across from me. An attractive woman walks in with a teapot on a silver tray, pours two cups of tea, and hands one to me than one to the Ambassador. Jean Claude told me to take whatever he offers, otherwise I will offend his hospitality. I would have preferred a beautiful Turkish woman for a dinner companion that evening, but all I got was this cup of tea. The Ambassador raises his cup toward me, says, "Serefe." Not sure what that means until he follows it with, "To honor." He turns, watches as the woman leaves the room. The door closes behind her before he turns to speak.

"Mr. Goemans speaks highly of you and says you can be trusted. I understand you have something to show me." I show him the two vests. He stands up, holds the white vest against his chest, then signals one of the guards to come over; he speaks to him in Turkish. The guard takes off his jacket , unstraps his holster which holds a huge gun. He slips into the blue suit vest, straps back on his holstered gun, puts his jacket over them both. The Ambassador hands me the white vest. "Dr. Hartman, please, put this one on." I take off my jacket, no gun, I must have forgotten it at the hotel, I put on the white bulletproof vest. He has his guard turn around to show off the vest beneath his jacket. I stand there with the white vest strapped over my shirt.

The Ambassador speaks again to the vested guard in Turkish, he hands the Ambassador his gun. He turns to me, the gun held to his side. "Would you mind if I test the vest right here?" I caution him, "Mr. Ambassador, you will damage the blue fabric over the Kevlar." He smiles, "No, I would prefer to test the vest you are wearing." I felt like my face might have turned as white as the vest, thinking this guy can miss and I'll be dead. Running through my mind ... deadly serious questions, "Did the Israelis actually check to make sure this thing will stop a bullet at this close range from a gun that large?" I feel like my life will end right here and now. My immediate thought is, "Damn you Jean Claude." So much of what I love in life also flashes through my mind.

The Ambassador raises the gun, but points it away from me and returns it to the guard. "If I do not return you to Mr. Goemans in the same condition you arrived, he will never forgive me... Tell me about prices and delivery." I feel as if I just literally dodged a bullet. I promptly take off the vest, we discuss the details of their possible purchase. He keeps the Kevlar blue suit vest, and says, "Tell Mr. Goemans I will be back to him in a few days." The gun-toting fullbacks escort me down that tiny elevator to the waiting car. I return to the Amigo Hotel in the same bodily condition as I left, but having experienced some temporarily accelerated heartbeats and flash memories of my life in the interim.

■ ■ ■

Shortly after my son was born, and during the time I was still consulting, another situation occurred which made me come to grips with my mortality. This time I had much more to lose. It shouldn't take such extreme situations to make us recognize the fragility of life. Maybe I'm fortunate to have had these experiences, because I've always held life dear, appreciating each healthy day. But for some reason I am not afraid of death; I wonder why?

One night I return from Manhattan after a dinner meeting, and stop by another consulting client who owns a Packaging Plus store in Queens. Billy, a hard-working guy of Greek ancestry, who I've been meeting with over the past month, also owns two fast food restaurants in Manhattan. He is looking to expand his businesses. We have a meeting scheduled for 9:00 PM, closing time at this Queens store. I drive by the store, park across the street, I see the front lights are out, but the lights in the back are still on, so I know Billy is still there waiting for me.

The front door is locked. I knock on the glass. Someone, it's too dark to see who, likely one of his employees, unlocks the door. The guy, now close up, has a ski mask over his head, grabs me by the front of my shirt, sticks a large silver handgun to the side of my head. "Keep ya mouth shut, do what I say, ya won't get hurt." With no other options, I'm thinking, "I want to see my son again," I follow his instructions. He drags me by my collar to the back room, pushes me to the floor beneath the packaging table. "Lay down, don't say a wud, don't move, or I swear I'll kill ya."

I see a second guy taking money from a register before I look behind me on the floor. There is Billy and his employee lying next to me beneath the table. Billy makes eye contact, pulls out his gun, places it under his other arm against the floor. He whispers, "If they're going to shoot us, I'm going to use it." Great, what a nice thought. Now, here I am at "The Under the Packaging Store Table Shoot-Out," instead of the "OK Corral." They'll never make a movie about this. I nod to Billy, figuring if they're going to shoot us, what the hell, maybe Billy is a good shot. What did I have to lose? Just everything!

One of the masked guys shouts, "Stay where ya are, count back from a hundred. One of ar guys is watchin from outside, he'll shoot ya if ya come out too soon." We maybe get to eighty before Billy crawls out, gets to his phone – no cell phones then – calls 911. "Billy, you think his gun was real? Think it was loaded?" Billy shrugs his shoulders, whispers up a cursing storm, he's really pissed they stole his money. I figure the gun is not real and that's why it was so big and silver. The police arrive in about ten minutes. They ask questions about the two guys right then and there, not like TV where they take you to the police station for questioning.

The plainclothes detective, notepad in hand, asks, "What were they wearing? Did you see a car? Anything special about their voices or the way they spoke? Did they wear gloves? Could you tell if they were white, black or Hispanic? Did they call each other by name?" Over the next hour he asks dozens of other questions. Finally, the detective in charge points to Billy's store employee and me, "You two can leave," He looks at Billy, "… but I still have a few more questions for you about what was taken."

He makes cold eye contact with the three of us. I know Billy's gun is still tucked away in his right side pocket. The detective shakes his head slightly from side to side, continues, "And by the way, you guys were lucky. Sounds like the pair we've been after. They pulled off two other robberies in the last month. Good thing you didn't do anything stupid. They killed a guy at the last place."

Guess the gun was real and loaded. I was so looking forward to reaching home that night and seeing Josh. I took a deep breath while watching him asleep in his crib, just thinking how much of his life I would have missed, to say nothing about my own.

■ ■ ■

Have you ever noticed how the topics of conversations evolve through various stages of life? Starting when I was a kid it was about teachers, homework, summer vacations, proms; then it was talk about colleges, courses, jobs or grad schools, and summer loves; moving on to marriage, babies, homes, paying bills, and vacations. I think some years after all the kids have left home and only the parents remain, health issues move to the forefront, with many conversations about medications, procedures and replacement parts. I can't help but remember Jay's title for these talks, "Organ Recitals."

So many of the guys I play tennis with have had knees and hips replaced, heart valves, open-heart operations, some even sport pacemakers. Fortunately I'm not in this group... yet. These replacements are so common that guys are pitching the club to set up a tennis tournament just for players with replacement parts. When some of these guys go through metal detectors, at airports, it must be like a cacophony of beeps, blinks and whistles.

As I age, the consequences of this aging process become more relevant to me, so I did some research. The Oak Ridge Atomic Research Center has determined about 98% of all the atoms in a human body are replaced every year. I apparently get a new suit of skin every month and a new liver every six weeks. And surprisingly, the lining of my stomach lasts only five days before it's replaced. The one thing I think is with me to stay are my bones, but no, new atoms have replaced all of my bones within the past year. Many experts go on to say there is a complete, 100% turnover of atoms in my body at least every five years. That means that not one single atom present in my body today was there five years ago. Doesn't this help explain why we look so different in our prime as compared to when we are a little or a lot older?

It only takes a little research to discover how challenging aging has become. Science has determined physical changes are built into our DNA. About 92% of older adults suffer from at least one of four aliments: heart disease, cancer, stroke or diabetes, and 77% have at least two of them. Our noses and ears get longer, or droop as we age, contributing to us looking more and more like Muppets. And like the generations before us, we become less tolerant of ignorance. We find it incredible when reasonably educated people do not know Israel is in the Middle East, Lincoln was a Republican, or the Earth revolves around the sun.

I think attitude has a lot to do with the rate at which we age. If we walk with a spring in our step, head erect, shoulders back as best we can, we contribute to our longevity. Even if it means a modest few more years or months, it will make us feel younger longer. This is a good thing. Being pessimistic must also be an aging accelerant as is frequent anger or a defeatist approach to issues. Positivity, without naiveté, I believe is a youthful stimulant.

There are consequences of aging we cannot change. Medical science says at about sixty, we need three times more light to see than a twenty year old needs. High-pitched sounds, like the voices of women and children, are harder to hear for older people, as are consonants. Talking louder doesn't much help; articulating consonants does. Every fifteen seconds an older person is treated in an emergency room for a fall, and about every thirty minutes one dies following a fall. It's been found that people who worry about falling seem to fall more often, so it's important to have a positive attitude toward bipedal mobility.

Some additional digging has yielded surprising health-related details about aging. Only about 5% of those over sixty-five suffer moderate to severe memory loss from Alzheimer's disease – I thought it was much higher. As we age, the discs between our backbones lose fluid, becoming thinner, making us shorter. This thinning in our neck vertebrae causes our heads to tilt slightly forward. The world is getting older, with the number of those over sixty expected to double from 2000 to 2050, from about 11% to 22% of the population, and those over eighty, quadrupling to about 400 million. I also found that nine out of ten people who reach the age of one hundred today are women. We have to get our male numbers up for those of us who reach one hundred, at least to five out of ten. Come on guys, we can do it! It's clear, healthcare is a key element of modern societies, with long-term care becoming an even more important component.

Memories, particularly distant ones, can be vivid in our aging minds. I remember picking berries on summer vacation when I was about ten. My grandmother gave me a pot to fill with blueberries and blackberries. And yet, I can go see a movie and the next day I may have some trouble remembering the title. Funny thing, our brains. When I think of the "Good Old Days" it's more often about when I was a kid, without any responsibilities.

I remember my mother telling my brothers and me, when we were very young, "Only brush the teeth you want to keep." She always tried to take the positive approach to parenting. This worked most of the time, but when there was a loose tooth and the Tooth Fairy was likely to be nearby, brushing around that tooth became an art.

I can think about some of the working years of my life if I concentrate, but it doesn't come as easy. I read a survey that found the two happiest times of peoples' lives are when they enter the workforce and when they retire. Maybe it's because that first paycheck is a validation of our worth, and I guess retirement is a kind of validation of our careers. As I get older, that sense of immortality is no longer in the eyes of my contemporaries. We all know we'll be facing the finish line of life sooner than later, and it can come upon us without notice. I hope it does for all of us.

As both a scientist and sci-fi writer, I'll miss the amazing and not so amazing innovations yet to be discovered, and what it will be like to live in the future. I'm sure there will be flying cars, driverless cars to take us everywhere, various electronic implants to make life easier, lots more robots doing many things people do today. All of these things are almost upon us now, certainly occurring during my lifetime. Imagine what things will be like in fifty, one hundred, and a thousand years from now. In 1940, just over 80 years ago, about one third of American homes did not have running water or indoor toilets; forty percent did not have showers or bathtubs and about sixty percent had no central heating.

Life today seems to be more complex, not simpler. Communication world-wide is instantaneous; an information and news overload. Media, prompted by profits, is drawn to the more horrific unsettling news to attract attention, and get readership and viewership. The world seems to be unraveling as evil people harm millions of others without the protection of moral, ethical and patriotic elected officials. Wars rage on driven by economics, ego, and religious differences. It is no wonder that many very senior people, near the end of their natural lives say, "We're getting out just in time."

■ ■ ■

"My wife and I go into town to visit a particular shop. When we come out, a policeman is writing out a ticket. We go up to him, I say, "Come on man, how about giving a senior citizen a break?"

He ignores us, continues writing the ticket. I call him an "asshole."

He glares at me, writes another ticket for having worn-out tires. My wife calls him a "shithead."

He finishes the second ticket, puts it on the windshield with the first. He writes more tickets. This goes on for about twenty minutes.

The more we abuse him, the more tickets he writes. He finally finishes, sneers at us, walks away.

Just then our bus arrives, so we get on it and go home. We always look for cars with campaign stickers we oppose.

We try to have a little fun each day now that we're retired.

■ ■ ■

One day a 80-year-old man arrives for his monthly checkup, and smiles when the doctor asks about his health.

"I have never felt better," says the old man, "I have taken a 20-year-old bride, and she is pregnant. What do you think of that?"

After a moment the doctor says, "Let me put it this way...I once knew a guy who was an avid hunter. One day he overslept, and in his rush to go out he took his umbrella instead of his rifle.

"When he got deep into the woods he suddenly came face to face with a huge bear.

"He raised his umbrella, pointed it at the bear and squeezed the handle. Do you know what happened then?"

"No, what happened?" replies the old man.

"The bear fell dead in front of him!" says the doctor.

"That's impossible," replies the old man, "somebody else must have been doing the shooting!"

"Now you got my point!" says the doctor.

■ ■ ■

Three old men are sitting on a porch. The first one says, "I wish I could take a healthy piss."

"I wish I could take a healthy crap," said another.

The third one admits, "I can take a crap at 6 AM and a piss at 11 AM. I just wish I could get up before noon."

16

THE LAST THANKSGIVING: LETTING GO

Maybe the hardest thing to deal with, as we get older, is watching parents become more helpless, knowing it won't be long before they are gone. When they are both gone, we become orphans. I have no parents on Earth to love me ever again. As our parents took care of us when we were babies and toddlers, they may drift down to needing a level of care to help them as they helped us. It won't take long to appreciate how hard this is for many parent-caregivers. I've seen it put a strain on the love between an adult child caregiver and their parents for the remainder of their lives, no matter how close they had been all the years before.

I think about my parents and how the process of losing them unfolded. My Dad was an athlete. He loved playing softball. He was a pitcher and was a switch hitter, being able to hit both lefty and righty. I always remembered him being in great shape, even though he was a heavy cigarette smoker. Back then, most everyone who returned from the war smoked. No one but the tobacco companies knew cigarettes would not only shorten lives, but for many, make those later years debilitating and often agonizing.

My earliest memory was when I was about three, living in a Quonset hut, in the Bronx. It had a half circle roof, like an arch, covered with galvanized steel sheets. There was one family living on each side, a common wall between the two units. There were two windows in the front of each unit.

One day while walking with my Dad, we find a homeless dog with three or four puppies. All but one is dead. My Dad explains how precious life is from the smallest living creatures to people. He takes the time to find a place we can dig a grave and bury those dead puppies. I insist we wait to make sure the dead puppies are not just sleeping before we bury them. None of them wake up. I finally accept their death.

Strange the things we remember. One of the other neighbors adopted the mother and her remaining puppy. We were moving to The Projects, also in the Bronx – no dogs allowed.

When I was about thirteen we moved to Wantagh on Long Island, into a Levitt house. There we got a Labrador mixed puppy, Corky, from the local pet adoption facility. I attended school in Levittown which was the adjoining town. My parents lived there for many years before my Dad decided to semi-retire and move to North Miami, Florida. Sometime before this final move he was already having breathing problems. It wasn't long before he was unable to work, on oxygen twenty-four hours a day, with full blown emphysema, a consequence of his cigarette smoking for forty years.

I am married when my parents move to Florida, still living on Long Island and working as a consultant. I return from a trip to Brussels, and a couple of days later our son is born. My dad is in intensive care when I call my Mom who is spending another day by his bedside in the hospital, as she has been doing for the last week. I tell her the baby's weight, time of birth, that he is perfectly healthy, and we've decided to name him Joshua. My Dad dies on May 6, 1982, the day after Josh is born.

My Mom assured me when she told him about Josh he smiled. I'm not sure she was telling me the truth, but it didn't much matter, as he was gone, and neither he nor Josh would ever get to meet each other.

■ ■ ■

During the war my Mom volunteered to join the Women Airforce Service Pilots (WASP) to fly planes to England and transport military aircraft for the war effort. When her father (my grandfather, Harry) found out, he stopped her from doing it. My parents got married during the war. When it was over my mother became a full-time housewife, eventually mother to five kids. When they moved to Florida, with my father's health failing, my mother studied to get a real estate license, then her broker's license to help support the family. She was about sixty then. Doug, my youngest brother, went to school at NYU and my sister was still at home. A couple of months after my Dad died, my grandmother Ester, Mom's mother, who had moved to Florida when my parents made the move, died.

I knew this young guy who was about twenty-three at the time, a talented artist, musician and songwriter. He attended NYU as did I, but I commuted from my home on Long Island. He was only there for one year when he was diagnosed as bipolar. After struggling with his med regimens, trying hard to concentrate on his studies, he could not handle it anymore and left school. He stayed a couple of months with his brother and his girlfriend who were living in Greenwich Village, right near NYU. He hung out with his college friends in the area and made new artist and music friends. He was always a gentle kind person before the bipolar behavior kicked into his life.

Then he went off his meds a second time and had an uncharacteristically angry incident in the city as he did the first time. In each case he was hospitalized for a mandatory three days for doctors to observe him, and provide a new regimen of drugs to manage his bipolar condition. He would go off his meds when he felt better. I remember he said, "I don't feel like myself. The meds drain away all my interest in drawing and music." His brother hoped things would get better, he would be able to manage his medication, and stay on an even keel for the future, especially with the stress of school off his mind. After being released this second time from the hospital, he left NYC and moved back home.

He got a local job near home and practiced his music and drawing. He made lots of new friends and seemed to be doing just fine. At least he did for a few months. But sadly he went off his meds again, and had another violent episode. Not that he hurt anyone, he would never do that, but he frightened his mother and her neighbors. The police were called, he was again put into a hospital for three days of observation and re-evaluation. He and his mother thought it best if he move out. One of his guitar-playing friends, who lived nearby, was happy to invite him to share his apartment.

Things seemed okay for a couple of weeks until the police arrived again at his mother's door. But this time it was to tell her that Doug had been found shot and had died. It was not a hold-up, or attack by someone in the area – he had shot himself. The officer explained he had lain down in the bathtub and used his friend's father's gun that was in the apartment. Seemed he did not want to make a mess so he shot himself lying in that tub. The officer handed her a note he had written. "Mom, I love you so much, and I am so sorry for all the trouble I have made for you and the family, love Doug." He was my youngest brother.

When Doug was still in NYC he spent a few weekends at my home on Long Island. He taught my son Josh to draw when he was only about four or five. One of my favorite pictures is Doug with Josh at a drawing board. I kept telling myself it wasn't true that Doug was gone and we would never spend time together again. I had just been down to see him and Mom a few weeks before.

I returned to Florida to be there for Mom at Doug's funeral. My brother Rick, three years younger than me, lived in northern Florida and drove down to North Miami. My other brother Fred flew in from New York City, and my sister Debra was there as well. Every day, for months, I would think about what I could have done differently to have prevented his death. I was the classic case of being depressed by continually trying to live the past, before his death.

There was no solace in knowing he was one of about 20,000 suicide gun deaths each year in the U.S. It was easy for me to come up with many things I thought I could have, should have, done differently, that might have made a difference, possibly preventing Doug's death. Probably none of it was true. It didn't matter because I could not go back and change anything. I now believe, having known more than one person who has died by suicide, that it's not always an act of weakness due to depression, but it could be one of strength. It's making a decision, a very difficult decision, one that is hard for others to understand or accept, especially by those loved ones left behind.

I have Doug's artwork and his picture in my office. I often think about him, what he would have done with his life. Today he would be fifty-three. Would he have a family, be a renowned artist or musician? No matter what he would have been, I would give almost anything to just hug him again. My brother Fred was very close to Doug, especially when they were both living in Manhattan while Doug attended NYU. They grew even closer when Doug lived with Fred in the Village between leaving school and returning home to Florida. I'm certain Fred became a psychologist, specializing in bereavement and PTSD, because of his time with Doug. In some indirect way, through Fred, Doug's influence has helped to relieve thousands of Fred's patients from so many of their life pains, hopefully giving them coping skills to deal with their losses.

My mother was a strong woman all her life, but this loss took a horrendous toll on her. She told me it was incredibly difficult losing my Dad, then her mother. But when she lost Doug, her child, it was crushing, almost more than she could bear.

■ ■ ■

She would lose another child several years later. My next oldest brother Rick, while serving two years in the Navy after high school, he had also become a heavy cigarette smoker like my Dad. He was on dialysis, waiting for a kidney transplant when my brother Fred and I went down to visit Mom in North Miami, then drove up to St. Augustine to visit Rick. We were all having lunch together near the St. Augustine pier when Rick's cell phone rang. He was told they had a kidney for him. It was particularly exciting because we were all together, sharing in the joy of the moment.

He had to get a checkup, a clean bill of health by his cardiologist, before he could accept the transplant. He was off to his doctors; we returned to North Miami to share the news with Mom. The cardiologist determined he needed heart surgery, a problem due to a consequence of his smoking.

That kidney had to be given to another recipient. The joy of that day dissolved into great disappointment for him and all of us. He would now have to continue on dialysis and go through a heart operation.

Rick never did have that heart operation. While preparing for it, they discovered he had an advanced case of lung cancer. Within a month of that diagnosis, with a one-day notice, having heard his condition had taken a serious turn, I flew down to Florida to be with him. Rick had large strong hands, was bigger and stronger than me, even though he was three years younger. He was now fifty-five, dying due to cigarette smoking, the same thing that killed my father at sixty-one.

I hold his warm hand by his hospital bedside. He's not responsive to my voice or my gentle squeezing of his hand. I talk to him, "Rick, I'm here, it's Steve. You've been a terrific father, to Vickie and Michael and a great brother… I love you, we all love you." Vickie sits on the other side of his bed holding his other hand.

She and her brother Michael were raised Catholic at the insistence of Rick's second wife, Barbara. Even though our family is Jewish, none of us are very religious, so Rick didn't much care. It was okay with him if it made Barbara happy.

Vickie repeatedly tells him he will soon be meeting another Jew who died about two thousand years ago. I'm sure she really believes this to be true and thinks it will comfort Rick. Without moving his lips or showing any expression on his face, if he can hear her, I think he is laughing inside. I'm sure she is hoping she too will meet Jesus when she dies, as her church has promised.

Fred's plane lands in Orlando, he gets in a rental car, drives to the St. Augustine Hospital to meet me and be with Rick. But no more than an hour after I arrive at Rick's bedside, I feel a distinct pulsing in his hand. Rick dies in this moment. His hand begins to cool almost immediately. That intangible, yet so important spark of life is gone. He is lifeless like that mother in Italy I stood next to so many years ago. Fred arrives after Rick dies. I've known Rick longer than anyone else in my life, except for my parents. I will never again see his great smile, hear his contagious laugh, or get to argue with him about politics. My life will never be the same, I will miss him so dearly. This moment punches a hole in my life that cannot ever be replaced. Mom takes it very hard, not only because he's her son, but because they both lived in Florida and Rick came to see her a couple of times each month. He and his daughter Vickie were her closest connection to the rest of the family since the rest of us all lived out of State.

Mom had remarried about ten years after my Dad died, and stopped her real estate work because her new husband wanted to travel. He told her he would cover all their expenses. They were married for about fifteen years when one day, at their community pool, across the street from their home, he had a heart attack and died. After Mom lived a couple more years in their home alone, we were fortunate that she and a woman friend, also a widow, both moved into an independent living facility, each with their own one bedroom apartment. It was great for her and the family. The facility provided two meals a day, weekly cleaning of her apartment, linen service, and a community of people with whom she could participate in various activities. The facility had a shuttle van to take residents shopping and to their doctor appointments.

■ ■ ■

On November, 22nd 2016, my wife and I arrive in Ft. Lauderdale a couple of days before Thanksgiving to spend it with Mom. We've scheduled a cruise that leaves Miami the day after Thanksgiving and goes through the Panama Canal, back to L.A. It's a great visit even though Mom is a little weak physically, but her mind is sharp. The following June she will celebrate her 95th birthday. Actually, the way I see it, the 95th anniversary of her birthday. We talk about politics, the latest about her grandchildren, and my brother and sister, both of whom will be down to Florida to see her over the next couple of months. We get Josh on the phone so Mom and he can talk. She loves talking to him, chatting about what's going on in his life.

She is in good spirits and says, tongue in cheek, "I want to move to L.A. so I can be closer to you." She knows it isn't possible for the many reasons I have discussed with her in the past, but I repeat them again,. "You now pay about $1,800 per month. You know I've checked places like yours in LA and they cost about $7,000-$8,000 per month for a studio, not a one bedroom like you have here." She knows this isn't even the most important issue. I ask her, as I have each time we have this discussion, "How do you like your doctors?" She always says, "I love them. They take such good care of me." I repeat what I have said many times before, "Okay, then, check with your doctors, if they are also ready to relocate to L.A., then we'll move you right out to California." We both have a laugh and move on to other interesting topics.

On Thanksgiving Day my wife and I take her to the restaurant of her choice to celebrate Thanksgiving – a Chinese restaurant. For me it's been a great few days. I tell her I'll come back to visit her for her 95th birthday anniversary in a few months, at the end of June. The day after Thanksgiving we stop by to see her on our way to the ship to say goodbye. The Oceania Cruise ship leaves that afternoon with the first stop in the Bahamas. The itinerary will take us to Colombia, through the Panama Canal, on to Costa Rica, Nicaragua, El Salvador, Guatemala, two stops in Mexico – Acapulco, Cabo – then north to San Diego, finally arriving in L.A.

My sister calls me when as we arrive in Guatemala to tell me Mom checked herself into the hospital because she was having some trouble breathing the night before. She has done this a couple of times before, over the past year, for her doctors to adjust her pacemaker or meds. I call her at the hospital, she sounds pretty good, "I'm okay, just a little trouble breathing last night and a little tired. I'll be getting home tomorrow or the next day." I call again the next day from Acapulco. Her aide, Maria, is by her hospital bedside, tells me she is asleep. Maria says if all the tests go well she will be home tomorrow or the next day, as expected. My sister calls again when we are in Cabo to tell me Mom died that morning. I have just had my last Thanksgiving with my Mom. I no longer have any parents. A profound sense of loss and loneliness overwhelms me.

Since my mother died, whenever I hear business promotions for Mother's Day, it reminds me I've lost her forever. I have long believed Mother's Day is every day I've had her in your life; the same for Father's

Day. This does not resonate as loudly as when they are gone. I'm not a fan of the commercialization of these days, even though they are reminders of how much we will miss them. Restaurants often double their prices compared to the days before and after these made-up holidays. In contrast, birthday celebrations for kids are exciting; they mark important steps to adulthood. But, as an adult, the anniversaries of my birth hold no special meaning for me. I don't celebrate them. My life feels more like a continuous journey, not distinct plateaus achieved each year.

Part of the price of life is losing friends and loved ones to death. Sudden tragic and accidental death, particularly for younger people, is most traumatic because it's like being cheated of years of wonderful life experiences. Those who loved them have had time with them stolen forever. These are the feelings I had when I lost my Dad who was only sixty-one, my brothers Doug at twenty-four, and Rick at fifty-five. There is still a little selfishness in feeling I wanted Mom to go on living, for me, for her, even though she was ninety-four and a half. Seems any time was too soon.

I've asked myself, *"What do I think it's like to be dead?"* I think this is what it's like; *Did you ever wake up after a good night's sleep not remembering a single dream? ...Well death is like sleeping without any dreams, except you don't wake up.* I don't believe dying is painful, if it's not due to trauma or severe illness. I see no reason to fear dying. I don't think many people do when it finally comes. It's not dying we fear, but rather stopping to live, no longer being with loved ones, doing the things that brought us joy and pleasure.

I remember my wife's aunt Sylvia telling me before her 97th birthday, "I'm tired. I'm ready to go." Her words came about a year after her husband of seventy years died, just months before his one hundredth birthday. This might have been a significant part of her desire to no longer hang on to life. She died three or four months later. Other friends have told me of hearing older relatives express this feeling of being tired and ready to go. Maybe we're a little like batteries that run out of energy. Finding ourselves requiring more sleep, naps, moving more slowly, taking joy in those activities that require the least amount of energy. Then there are those less fortunate who are racked with pain when they awake each morning and sadly telling themselves, *"Now I have to live through another day."* If death does not happen suddenly, without notice, free of pain or suffering, then I think being tired and ready to go is the best way to leave this wonderful experience we call life.

■ ■ ■

An attorney gathers the entire family for the reading of the will. Relatives come from near and far, to see what has been left to them in the bequests. The lawyer somberly opens the will, begins to read:

"To my cousin Ed, I leave my ranch.

To my brother Jim, I leave my money market accounts.

"To my neighbor, and good friend, Fred, I leave my stocks.

"And finally, to my cousin George, who always sat around, never did anything, but wanted to be remembered in my will, I say, "Hi, George.""

■ ■ ■

Unable to attend the funeral after his father dies, a son who rarely visited his father and left much of his care to his brother, calls his brother, tells him, "Do something nice for Dad and send me the bill."

He gets a bill for $200, which he pays.

The next month, he gets another bill for $200, which he also pays, figuring it was some incidental expense.

Bills for $200 keep arriving every month.

Finally the man calls his brother again to find out what is going on.

"Hey brother, what's with these $200 bills coming every month?"

"Well," says the other brother, "you said to do something nice for Dad. So I rented him a tuxedo."

17

LIFE IS STILL FULL OF SURPRISES

The most recent assault on my life came about ten years ago when I was diagnosed with cancer. I had an elevated PSA during one of my regular annual checkups so my doctor sent me to a urologist for a biopsy. The result was Stage I cancer. When the urologist met with my wife and me to discuss his findings, he immediately outlined how he would operate, remove my prostate, and I would be "*cancer-free.*" I guess this is the cash-out phrase, "cancer-free." Sounds simple but there was a catch. In fact several BIG catches. And it wasn't even true that he would be sure I was going to be "cancer-free."

Even using the new robotic surgery techniques, the chance of me becoming impotent was about 50%; the chance of incontinence, leaking urine, needing a diaper, about 20%. I told him I was not a fan of hospitals and would evaluate all the alternatives before deciding whether to have surgery. I researched all available information I could find, then brought my newly discovered diagnosis to one of our "Organ Recitals."

Over coffee, before getting on the courts with several tennis buddies at the club, I find out a number of them had prostate cancer. Mike B says, "Before you do anything see Richard, my oncologist in Marina Del Rey." I make an appointment with Richard for the first appointment he has available.

The following week I am in Chris' office, a well-respected radiologist in Beverly Hills to get another opinion. He enters his offices with my records in hand. My wife and I are there for the consultation. He says, "Steve, I'm not going to make any money on you today... You had a very small amount of cancer and it doesn't appear to be the aggressive kind. I recommend you find an oncologist and just do 'Watchful Waiting.' With a Gleason score of six (3 & 3), if you're lucky, you may never need surgery or radiation."

Firstly, I'm not a lucky person, but I like his advice. As we leave he adds, "A urologist is like a hammer, everything he sees looks like a nail, and in this case that nail is the surgical removal of your prostate."

About a week later I met Richard, the prostate oncologist recommended by Mike B. He prescribed a daily med, finasteride. I saw him every four months for an exam and PSA test. A couple of years later, I saw him every six months. This continued for about nine years. Nothing changed over this time, most importantly, I had no concern about the consequences of surgery. I had a PSA test twice a year, periodic sonograms and another biopsy.

Then I'm told the last thing I want to hear. One of my blood tests shows an elevated PSA. This could be a false positive. It can happen if a man has sex within forty-eight hours prior to the PSA test, or has a mild case of prostatitis, an infection of the prostate. To double check if there is really a problem, if the cancer is indeed growing, Richard does a sonogram. He detects a small increase in the tumor lodged in my prostate. Again, to be totally sure, he sends me for an MRI. All these tests finally lead me to needing the definitive test again, another biopsy. The most uncomfortable and unpleasant of all tests. Richard suggests I use a doctor in Ventura who has developed a new process for treating prostate cancer by freezing which I may want to consider if necessary.

The results of that biopsy are not what you write home about. The tumor has grown and was now a Gleason seven (four and three) Stage II cancer. I had avoided this decision for many years. I now have to come face to face with the potential of destroying the quality of my remaining life with one of the treatments, or cutting it short with a premature, and very uncomfortable prostate cancer death. Unfortunately, there is no third option.

It's easy to say, "Why me?" but just as fair to ask, "Why not me?" About three million men in the U.S. are diagnosed with prostate cancer each year; one dies every twenty minutes. So for me, the time for action was now. My mother had already lost two children, so unless she was about to lose me, while she was still alive, I would never tell her. She died never knowing I had cancer.

On another beautiful sunny day in Marina Del Rey I meet with Richard at his offices to review and discuss my options, based on this new reality. He starts the conversation by saying, "I can only lay out the options, but it has to be your decision." I know this can be the most important decision for the rest of my life. "How much time do I have before I must do something?" Richard looks up, "No longer than thirty to sixty days to reduce the chance of it spreading beyond the prostate." Okay, now this is getting serious. I look directly at Richard. "What if I choose to do nothing?"

By his expression, my question surprises him. He responds immediately, "If it grows slowly, you'll have about ten years maybe more, maybe less, but it can begin to grow more rapidly at any time, no way of knowing." I think to myself, the good news about doing nothing is there will be no horrible side effects during those years. The bad news is, dying of prostate cancer can be painful and very unpleasant, to say nothing about it cutting short my life. Over these past nine years I am thinking treatments have improved. "Tell me what's new about how they treat prostate cancer." Richard is clear, "There has been some improvement, but the negative consequences have not been eliminated, just somewhat reduced."

"What are my choices and the real chances of each of them screwing up my life?" Richard closes my file, sits back. "During surgery there's a one-half percent chance of dying, probably the same as undergoing any surgery under general anesthesia. There's about a 2% to 5% chance of some degree of incontinence." Immediately the image of me wearing a diaper on the tennis courts comes to mind. Not a pretty picture. Clearly not a good quality of life option. He continues. "There's somewhere between a 30%-40% chance of impotence, even though surgeons claim it's only 20%.

But drugs like Viagra and Cialis can reduce this, in many people, by as much as 50%." Damn! Not all people, just many people. This means my chance of impotence is between 15% and 20%. If I'm lucky enough to be among those "many people." Again I remind myself I'm not a very lucky person.

I'm thinking, if I end up impotent I don't think I want to continue to live. Sex is that important to me. Doing nothing is now becoming a potentially more viable option. Maybe in ten years, or in as many years as I have left, they will have better meds to deal with end of life prostate cancer, or maybe even a cure. I then ask, "What are my alternatives to surgery?" Richard is calm and thorough, one of the reasons I have always had confidence in being his patient. "There's freezing. Based on your recent biopsy, your cancer qualifies as a good subject since it's located on only one half of your prostate. They freeze that half, it kills the cancer, then we monitor the other half like we did these past nine years. The urologist who did your biopsy, also developed this process, and indicates in a recent article that there's about a 20% chance of impotence, about a 1% chance of incontinence."

That reduced chance of impotence has my attention. The lower chance of incontinence, at first blush, is a winner. I'm not sure I like having to watch the other half of my prostate for the rest of my life, visits every six months, periodic sonograms, MRI's and the dreaded biopsies. If I had cancer in one half of my prostate, I'm guessing I'll get it in the other half, then I'll be back to this decision again. "How long has he been doing these procedures?" Richard closes his laptop, "His article cited three years of studies but I think he's been doing it for four or five years." Now I'm thinking that's not so long. Maybe his 20% is not so accurate since I'm sure he hasn't performed this procedure on thousands of patients to get a good sampling.

I make another appointment with Chris in Beverly Hills, who nine years ago recommended "Watchful Waiting." He checks all my tests, agrees with Richard, it's time to choose a treatment. "We can do either beam radiation or radioactive seeds." I've heard of both but have never been too interested in the benefits of one or the other, until now. "So what are my chances of side effects?" I'm getting right down to what matters most. "Steve, they are about the same for seeds or beam radiation – about a 2% chance of incontinence and about a 30% chance of impotence." I still don't like my chances of becoming impotent. "What's involved with both?" He tells me, "With seeds we place radioactive seeds in your prostate. With traditional radiation, you will need to be radiated every day for about five and a half weeks, except weekends. Each treatment takes about fifteen minutes, it's all external." Since radiation has a long history of success, and I don't like hospitals or invasive medical procedures, and I trust Chris, external radiation seems like a possible option to doing nothing.

Chris adds, "It's common for this radiation regimen to be followed by hormone therapy, for a relatively short period of time, to help ensure that all the cancer has been eliminated." Now this strikes a bad note for me. Short of surgery and hospital stays, I have read hormone therapy is not a walk in the park. It often comes with many additional unpleasant side effects. Just three include hot flashes, loss of interest in, or inability to have sex, and weakened bones. What a basket of joy this would be, especially if I was unlucky to be in the 30%, after radiation, ending up with the dreaded impotence. I tell Chris, "I don't want to do hormone therapy, it's a deal killer."

I tell Chris we must find a way to avoid this. Together we come up with something he has not done before, which will now require my approval to avoid any legal exposure for him and his practice. Of course I agree, because impotence to me is a death sentence. We agree on a unique treatment protocol. It will involve radiating the current cancer with 120% of the typical radiation level he intends to use on the rest of my prostate. He tells me, "I need to warn you, the side effects of radiation will be more uncomfortable by increasing the radiation over the twenty-eight days of treatment." I'm okay with that if I avoid hormone therapy. I sign the release forms.

The 30% chance of impotence weighs heavy on my mind, even though for many people, not all, it can be reduced by 50% with drugs to about 15%. While I love so many things about living, I cannot imagine continuing without the great pleasure of sexual intercourse. Studies have found orgasms stimulate every part of the brain, so this may suggest why scientists, mathematicians, numbers people are more likely than others to benefit from this orgasmic stimulation. I've read several biographies of brilliant science and math people which all noted their very active libidos, including Einstein. I have no factual data, but I'm guessing it's true. While I am not nearly as brilliant as those who have had biographies written about them, I am of the science and math type mind.

A neighbor's three-legged dog comes to mind, knowing I'm just playing a mind game with myself. This little white dog has so adapted to missing one rear leg, to watch it walk and run, one would think it didn't know one leg is missing. I'm no dog; I would know what I was missing if I became impotent. I don't think I would be able to adapt, it would make life unbearable. On the positive side, I force myself to focus on my 70% chance of not becoming impotent. If I become impotent, and drugs don't help, then I still can make a final decision about going forward.

I start the month of radiation treatments on a Wednesday with a twenty-minute drive to Wilshire Boulevard in Beverly Hills. A rather simple process begins once I enter the radiation room through a one-foot-thick iron or lead door. I lay face up on a carbide platform which will allow radiation to pass through my body, even from beneath me. My jeans and undershorts are dropped around my ankles; a towel covers my genitals, just below where the beam of radiation will penetrate through my abdomen into my prostate. This huge machine moves over my body, rotates around and under me until returning to where it started. Then it does the same maneuver but in the opposite direction, covering the same 360-degree path. The beam is focused on my prostate gland but will pass through whatever is in its way. This is why there are potential side effects to the rectum, colon, urethra, and the urinary bladder.

I'm advised to take a teaspoon of Metamucil twice a day to help avoid diarrhea. After each treatment they ask if I have experienced blood in my urine or stool, pain when urinating, diarrhea, or more frequent urination during the day or at night, causing me to get up from sleep more often. Each time I'm about to have sex I'm concerned the last time I did it, could have actually been my last time. Or that this may be the last time I have sex for the rest of my life. Fourteen days into the treatments, I have none of the side effects except for pain urinating. The pain level is at about four on a scale of ten, but by the end of the treatments, it's closer to an eight. The pain is most acute when urination begins, then there's a constant burning sensation at about a pain level of four. I tell myself I can live with this, so long as it is the only cost of radiation, without suffering from incontinence or being impotent.

One month after the radiation ends, I'm not incontinent or impotent. My PSA score goes from a 3.5 down to 3.0. This is good. I had to go for checkups every three months with Richard for a PSA blood tests during the first year, and then every four months. At the end of almost two years after radiation treatment my PSA goes down steadily from 3.0 to 1.38, 1.08, 0.60, 0.45, 0.42 to 0.28. If all is well, the PSA should continue at this level, maybe a little lower. My next checkup will make sure it continues to go down or stay down. If the cancer is gone, it's gone, right? No, not right. If the PSA rises more than 2.0 points from its lowest score, before I die, the cancer had left my prostate before we killed it with radiation, and moved to another part of my body. If we don't detect such an increase in the next four years it is then unlikely to be present. Richard tells me I have a 30% chance of the cancer returning during this time.

I met Rod in Chris' waiting room before many of my treatments. He was also getting radiation treatments for prostate cancer. This would not be noteworthy except for the fact this was his third time having a series of treatments; he had his prostate surgically removed about 10 years earlier. That's right, surgically removed. Even taking this extreme and seemingly complete approach to eliminating his cancer, it still could be lurking somewhere in the body. And during a conversation with a good friend at tennis, at those ongoing Organ Recitals, he told me about a friend of his who had his prostate removed about twenty years ago and recently died from prostate cancer in his bones.

Good thing I don't worry. If I have a problem I either deal with it or forget it. I have dealt with this potential attack on my life. Other than periodic checkups, which I think make sense, I'm done thinking about it.

If there comes a time I must deal with it again, I will, but until then, I have a lot of living to do.

■ ■ ■

A wife comes home late one night, quietly opens the door to her bedroom. From under the blanket, she sees four legs instead of just her husband's two.

She reaches for a baseball bat, starts hitting the blanket as hard as she can. Once she's done, she goes to the kitchen to have a drink.

As she enters, she sees her husband there, reading a magazine.

He says, "Hi darling, your parents have come to visit us, so I let them stay in our bedroom. Did you say hello?"

■ ■ ■

An 85-year-old man is requested by his doctor to get a sperm count as part of his physical exam.

The doctor gives him a jar, says, "Take this jar home, bring back a semen sample tomorrow."

The next day the 85-year-old man reappears at the doctor's office and gives him the jar, which is still empty.

The doctor asks what happened and the man explains.

"Well, Doc, it's like this; first I tried with my right hand, then with my left hand, but still nothing.

"I asked my wife for help. She tried with each hand, then with her mouth, still nothing.

"We even called up Arleen, the lady next door, she also tried; first with both hands, then she even tried squeezin' it between her knees, but still nothing."

The doctor was shocked! "You asked your neighbor?"

The old man replied, "Yep, none of us could get the damn jar open."

■ ■ ■

A pastor of a church is sitting in his study when the phone rings.

"Hello, is this Reverend Jones?" the caller asks.

"It is." replied the pastor.

"This is Bill Johnson with the Internal Revenue Service. I was wondering if you could answer a few questions?"

"I'll try." said the pastor.

"Do you know a John Timmons?"

"I do."

"Is he a member of your congregation?"

"He is."

"Did he donate $10,000 to the church?"

"He will."

18

FUNERALS AND MEMORIALS

Entering life as a newborn is easy – it's all on our parents – but leaving is more complicated - it's all on us. Even before we die, a responsible person makes it easier on loved ones, by having a Will and an Advanced Healthcare Directive (Living Will). A Will is all about what we have left-over after living, who gets it, and our final wishes on how to dispose of our body after we're dead. Most people leave all they have to their spouse, significant other, and/or children. The wealthier you are the more of a problem this seems to be. How many movies, TV shows, or news article about family infighting and turmoil have you seen about poor or middle class families? This must be some sort of social payback for the wealthy.

A Living Will can get complicated. You choose someone to make decisions about the life you have left, when you can't make decisions for yourself. This could be the first rub in our exit strategy. Who to choose? Remember, when and if a critical, near-death decision needs to be made, it will not be by majority vote, or a committee of ex-wives or children. No, you must pick one person. For me, I want to be confident this person will not only do what I wish, but will have the presence of mind and judgement to make a decision in a crucial moment while I'm still alive. I don't want to be resuscitated if my survival results in me bordering on a vegetable, and I mean no disrespect to vegetables.

This person, in consultation with my doctors, and family must make this decision, even if others in my life disagree. This person must be strong enough to live with themselves if they make the wrong decision, either by letting me die or keeping me alive, and finding out later it was a mistake. I choose my brother Fred.

Then of course you need backups, just in case your first choice dies before you. You can change these choices while you are still of sound mind. If someone picks their wife, then goes through a hateful divorce, you can see a change would be prudent.

Our Will can relieve our survivors of the burden to decide if we will be buried, cremated, or even frozen. Burials cost between $8,000 to $12,000, some less, others much more. I guess it ranges in cost like weddings. I think costly funerals are a waste of money, much like the primitive practice of the Pharaohs who buried gold and other treasure for their afterlife. I found there is so much involved in burials it boggles my mind. The basic fee is only about $2,000, but this is just the start. There is a host of additional costs: removal and transfer of body, body preparation, embalming, cost of facility, staff during funeral services, printed materials, flowers, the hearse for the casket, burial vault, headstone, opening and closing fees. A lot to deal with…

But let's not forget the grave plot. Some people will seek a site with a nice view for themselves when preplanning their funeral. The dead person is below ground, the view to be had will be the same as from a windowless basement. But others get the view location to encourage visitors. Are they expecting visitors to picnic? Do they think they will be lonely, but a good view will bring conversational visitors? Are these people crazy? They will be dead!

This is not lost on cemeteries which I'm sure charge premiums for plots with a view. A plot is an expensive land purchase. The average plot is three feet by nine feet; twenty-seven square feet of land. If it only costs $1,000, this is the equivalent of $1,615,000 per acre. And if it cost $2,000 this brings the land cost equivalency up to about $3,250,000 per acre. So I guess the cemetery business is a pretty good business, yet it's ironic that cemeteries in the U.S., like people, have a limited life, ending when they run out of land.

Another key element of this death march, burying treasure for the afterlife, is the casket. They come in all different materials: metal caskets cost from $3,000 to $50,000 for bronze, soft woods under $1,000, hard woods $2,000 to $3,000, fiberglass or polymers cost much more. I guess it depends on how much money a family wants to, or can afford to bury. Some caskets last longer than others; does it really matter? Then of course there is the lining and cushioning of the casket, which I guess is for the comfort of the dead person. Do people really believe the body will know the difference? This seems insane. Is this just me?

Then there is the popular alternative to burial – cremation. A "Direct Cremation" can cost less than $1,000; they average about $1,000 to $2,000. The body is put in an oven, heated to 1600–1800 degrees for a few hours, reducing it to between four to six pounds of ashes. About 50% of people in the U.S. choose cremation, while in Britain, about 70% choose this option. Americans will soon be as frugal as the Brits. It's been reported that by 2030 the choice for cremations in the U.S. will be up to about 80%.

I first thought cremation was much better for the environment by not taking up space on the planet. Then I realized there is a large waste of energy during cremation with all that heat required to create the ashes. I found out the human body contains 219 toxic pollutants, including preservatives, pesticides, and heavy metals like lead and mercury, all of which are released into the air. The decomposition of a body in the ground also leaches these same toxic bodily chemicals; some may reach into ground-water below cemeteries. So let's call it a draw, thus leaving the choice to personal preference and disposable money.

When I think about being buried, the image of maggots and worms, bacteria, etc. eating at my body until it's gone, seems undesirable. Being turned into ash doesn't conjure up any better of a feeling. Of course this kind of thinking is ridiculous. When I'm dead I won't feel either one. There will be no thoughts or feelings, so who cares? Why bury or burn thousands of dollars your surviving family or friends can use to enjoy what's left of their lives? But what if someone wants to visit your remains after you're dead? Seems an urn of ashes works best. It's portable, and can be kept at home or moved around the country if need be. Ashes can be spread out illegally on Rodeo Drive in Beverly Hills, or legally in a favorite body of water off Santa Monica or Cabo, or maybe in the desert. Visiting can be as easy as going shopping or on vacation, at a much lesser cost than purchasing a residence for the body at a cemetery. So there it is, a clear reason to go with cremation.

■ ■ ■

For the science-minded, like myself, cryogenic suspension with liquid nitrogen has an initial appeal. Many people have chosen to be frozen when they die, to be revived in the distant future, maybe fifty to one hundred years from now, when science can safely defrost their bodies and fix whatever had caused their death. While some freeze their entire body, others take the more economical alternative, just freeze their heads. This head thing seems logical, since who we really are is *all in our heads*. If they can bring us back, they should be able to give us a better body.

Can someone be safely frozen and actually revived? A possible indication might be the freezing of fertilized eggs. When defrosted and implanted in a uterus, they can develop into healthy children, but here we are only talking about several cells, not fully mature bodies. Unfortunately no warm-blooded animal has ever been frozen then brought back to life. This does not bode well for my confidence in coming out the other end of this process when defrosted. What about the cost for this shot at a second life? The least costly service I found will do whole body cryopreservation for $28,000. Other companies charge from $80,000 for heads only, to about $200,000 for whole bodies. One cryonics company has someone who has been frozen since 1967. If they defrost this guy now, and can't bring him back to life, or can't fix what killed him, it would literally "kill" their chances of selling their services. So frozen he stays. While these services admit they can't guarantee success, their sales pitch is, *"There's one thing we can guarantee, if you don't sign up for cryonics, you will have no chance at all of being revived in the future."* A good point!

But if it works, all the people I love, including my son, who would have outlived me if he has a normal life span, will have died. Also, I am unlikely to easily adapt to the advances that will have taken place while I was frozen. Not having followed the learning curve as technology developed, technological developments will be far beyond what I had been accustomed to in my previous life, maybe more than I can grasp. This does not seem to be a good alternative. I may have to just go with traditional death. Imagine that, choosing old-fashioned regular death. But I do want to live my life to the max, using up my full supply of life the best I can, even if it's just in the adequate body I have today.

But what about reincarnation, is it really a possibility? I'm not sure I want to start over – being a baby, then toddler, elementary school kid, middle school kid, then a high schooler. This would be a nightmare. Growing up the first time was hard enough. Happily I didn't realize it back then. It might be good to come back as a person in my twenties or thirties, but nobody is going to give up their body for me. What if I come back as a female? That would be weird, especially if I have any memory of being me. Worst of all, what if I come back as a baby born in a third-world country where starvation and early death is more common than living a healthy happy life with all the luxuries we have here in the U.S.? This thought is not only troubling; it makes me more empathetic toward all of those who are suffering around the world today. It would be like being in purgatory and suffering throughout my short life.

The reason reincarnation even remotely flashes in my mind is because of the feeling I sometimes have had when I've visited historic places like Greece, Rome and Pompeii. There is a stirring within me that suggests a familiarity, as if I had been in this place before. Also, as a kid I was a natural with a bow and arrow, and at a young age I did exceedingly well in the Nassau County archery contest. So, at least then, in my fourteen year old mind, I thought that maybe I used a bow and arrow in a previous life. But logic and additional education has brought me to realize reincarnation is not possible. More bizarre is that some people think they may come back as another animal or plant. As far as I'm concerned, it's just a fantasy. Not unlike the fantasy of going to heaven after death.

I'm also certain those who died before us are not waiting to greet anyone in heaven. They are not looking down on us, they're not anywhere but gone. They have no physical or working eyes, bodies or minds, and there is no undiscovered area of space between the Earth and the moon where heaven is hidden. This belief in heaven gives comfort to many people who look forward to their dearly missed loved ones waiting to greet them when they die. Maybe for many it's a way of not fearing death. For these people, like children who believe in Santa Claus or other mythical characters, it provides comfort in an often difficult world. Even this good thing can be turned into a vile obsession for the followers of fanatical religious extremists, causing them to carry out inhuman acts during their lives, falsely believing they will be rewarded in a happier after-life.

Why are people so good at heaping praise, loving thoughts, and the warmest feelings upon the dead at funerals and memorials, but so bad at doing it with their loved ones while they're still alive?

■ ■ ■

How many times have you attended a funeral, hearing what is said by the rabbi, priest, or friends, makes you think you're at the wrong service? If not for recognizing people attending who are associated with the dead person are you grounded to believe you are in the right place. What is said about dead people doesn't always match the sometimes mean-spirited, dishonest, inconsiderate bastard you knew. This reminds me of the funeral and services for Abee. I heard the rabbi and then his daughter speak in such glowing terms as to the loving relationship she and her father had. While I sat there, the images and words of that night at their home over dinner raced through my mind. Had I just heard their words at the service, without seeing who was saying them, the very last person I would have guessed they were talking about would be Abee.

Larry, also a friend at the tennis club, was the manager for Bette Midler, Robin Williams, Billy Crystal and Woody Allen. He didn't tell any of us he had cancer. He took boxing lessons to stay in shape and yet he had a bit of large belly. I remember I once asked him over coffee, before we went out to play tennis, "How you doing today?" He replied as he smoothed over his stomach with his hand, "I'll be doing much better when this swelling goes down." When he entered the hospital we didn't know until after he had died. He chose to keep his dying very private and personal. There was a memorial service with lots of Hollywood types there, many people spoke about this real guy.

This hypocrisy can stop. Prepare your own comments for your service. Do it as a video or audio recording, or just put it on paper and have a person *you select* read it to those who have taken the time to attend. Give it a try, write one up for yourself. It will hopefully need several revisions as you live on for many years... but we never know, do we? It will be the last thoughts the people who care about you will ever hear *from you*.

■ ■ ■

I will have my brother Fred read mine at my memorial service, if there is one. Part of what I would have him read once my life ends is this:

"Thanks to all of you who are here today. I wish I could be there. I'm guessing by my absence, and this being read, my death came as a complete surprise to me. I would not have wanted it to happen any other way. I'm sorry I'll not be able to spend more time with my family and friends. Just walking beneath a California blue sky, feeling the warmth of the sun, breathing the air, was such a pleasure. I'm particularly thankful to those people I had spent the most time with in my life. I really enjoyed playing tennis with the dozen-plus men and women at the club. While winning was always good, I looked forward, a few days each week, to just being out there on the courts playing the best I could. I often played pretty well, but on some days I would lose concentration. My mind would wander to other interesting and wonderful things in my life. During those lapses, all was not lost for me, but sadly it would cost my partners some games or a set. Sorry about that. I particularly enjoyed spending time with the guys over lunch at the Nineteenth Hole. Whether the conversation was about politics, sports (I could only participate when it came to tennis), or the trials and tribulations of life, it was always a comfortable place to unwind.

"My neighbors were a daily joy to meet while walking our dog Harry. We'd often see Gene with "Baby," his dog and Irv with "Lulu." Also George and Graziella would often sit on their first-floor terrace, greet me when I came home, or Harry and I would stop before their terrace for a short talk about one thing or another. Tom, my comedic neighbor, was always in a happy mood, often ready to share one of his many jokes when we met. I also enjoyed and benefited from spending time with my Malibu writing friends at Bonnie's house and those other writing friends who I've met and worked with over the years. The casts and crews of my films and the stage show also enriched my life. I often reminded myself of these people while I was alive, because I wanted to appreciate them when I could. John my co-broker for over thirty-five years was always a privilege to work with, as a professional and my good friend.

"I assure you all, I will not be looking down on any of you, because I'm dead, no longer existing on or off planet Earth. I felt so lucky to have been born in the U.S., to have had the great life I did, free of war, starvation or other deprivations hundreds of millions of other humans have had to endure during their lives. I'm sure you all feel the same."

I will then talk about my family and a number of milestones in my life that made it a pleasant and enjoyable experience. I will touch upon some of the disappointments which contrasted with the great things in my life.

"There are regrets I have when I honestly and critically review my life. I have made lots of good decisions and some bad ones, but I don't think I'm much different than any one of you. One thing I particularly regret, is not spending more time with my Dad, Norman, especially in the last months of his life. I should have created the time for him instead of permitting excuses of life to get in the way. There is never a chance to make up for such lost opportunities when death is so final. He died on May 6th, 1982, the day after our son Josh was born. I hope he was lucid enough, in his last hours of life, to have shared in the joy of Josh's birth.

I wish I had thanked my Dad and Mom more often for all the good things they did, and for the struggle my parents endured in their lives to care for my brothers and sister as we were growing up. Yes, I told Mom each time we spoke on the phone, and whenever I saw her, I loved her, but I didn't thank her enough, or express my admiration for how hard she worked for our family. Not for the strength she demonstrated and heartache she suffered when she lost my father, and my two brothers."

I would end with some final thoughts such as:

"I loved living. But I won't miss it. We are all exempt from experiencing the pain of this loss of life, since when we are dead, we have no idea what we are missing. My life was merely a blink in time compared to human life on our planet. But it's all any of us have.

I wish all of you a great rest of your lives and hope you find pleasure in every day. I strongly suggest you acknowledge all those around you who help to make your life as wonderful as it is, before they or you are no longer around to share a joke, a smile, hug, kiss, or love. And when you cross the finish line at the end of your lives, as I have, I wish it comes as a sudden surprise, and if not, that you do not suffer during your last few strides to your finish line."

■ ■ ■

A woman's husband dies. He has $20,000 to his name. After paying all the funeral expenses, she tells her closest friend there is no money left.

The friend asks, "How can that be? You told me he had $20,000 a few days before he died. How could you be broke?"

The widow replies, "Well, the funeral cost me $6,500. And, of course, I had to make the obligatory donation to the church, pay the organist and all. That was $500, and I spent another $500 for the wake, the food and drinks.

"The rest went for the memorial stone."

The friend asks, "$12,500 for the memorial stone? My God, how big was it?"

The widow replies, "Three carats."

■ ■ ■

A man and a friend are playing golf one day at their local golf course. One of the guys is about to chip onto the green when he sees a long funeral procession on the road next to the course.

He stops in mid-swing, takes off his golf cap, closes his eyes, and bows his head down in prayer.

His friend says: "Wow that is the most thoughtful and touching thing I have ever seen. You truly are a kind man."

The man then replies: "Yeah, well we were married 35 years."

EPILOGUE

One day I will no longer walk into my kitchen, living room or bedroom, nor on the streets by my home, in this city, or upon this Earth. If I'm lucky, the end will be a surprise to me, one I'll never recover from. I will leave others behind who I have loved and who have loved me, or at least liked me. They will continue on a path to their own finish lines, the same end everyone before them and everyone after them will cross.

Our lives are like footprints in the sand; an impression left in just a moment in time and then gone. We will all follow the great people in history who have died before us. Their imprints in the memory of humanity will be deeper, more defined, and longer lasting. Every one of us will leave an impression with those we shared time with, and for those for whom our existence mattered. We will all be remembered even if it's for only their lifetimes. Every life is significant, and all are remembered by someone for some amount of time.

I've lived my life doing almost everything I wanted to do, maybe not seeing every part of our planet I wished I could, but always trying to do it by not hurting people or other living things along the way. It's my life to live my way, within the parameters I have set for myself. I have chosen to share it with some people but not to forfeit it to anyone. This is my only chance at life and I am dedicated to making it as pleasurable as possible.

If I can bring joy and pleasure to others along the way, it will make my journey all that much better.

■ ■ ■

Black Holes hurl through the universe; the very smallest ones, the size of atoms, go undetected. What happens if one the size of a nickel, also undetectable, having a mass greater than that of the Earth, flies into our solar system, strikes Earth? In an instant, all animal life, plant life, water, and dirt on the surface of Earth will immediately disappear, sucked into a huge gravitational vortex. Nobody on the planet will have even a second to scream. Then the entire Earth will be drawn into this Black Hole. It could happen at any moment...

I believe every minute I'm alive is a celebration for the appreciation of this special existence I share with others. I do everything I can to soak up the pleasures afforded me in this life, since I don't know how many days, months or years remain. The end may not involve an encounter with a Black Hole or other cosmic event, out of our control and undetectable. It may just be my expiration date or an unfortunate accident.

Maybe as a physicist I appreciate more than most people the fragility of our tiny planet in the vastness of our universe; the cosmic events that can snuff us out like a candle in an unexpected instant. Or being able to see the slow death to our planet and humanity being caused by myopic thinkers among politicians and business people focused on their short-term gains.

I have wondered when I die if I will miss doing the things I like so much – spending time with friendly acquaintances, those I care about and love? The answer is of course NO... I will not be able to miss anything, or anyone, since I will have no thoughts when I'm dead.

Those who die leave the pain of missing them, thoughts of what could have been, to the living. Death is so much harder on the living. This reminds me to do all those things I love doing, to spend as much quality time with those I love and care about, while I still can. How about you?

■ ■ ■

I think this is a great take on a good life:

> In the end only three things matter:
> How much you love
> How gently you live, and
> How gracefully you let go of things not meant for you.
> Buddha

There are circumstances thrust upon us that will help shape the directions we take and what we do in life. We will have plenty of choices to make, interests to follow, people to share our experiences, and we must not deny ourselves opportunities by being shy, apprehensive, or too inhibited to grab life's benefits making this life of ours, not just okay, but incredible. For me a summer job led to medical school in Italy; the draft drove me into the field of education; a course on birds got me to fly and soar like a falcon; tennis friends launched me into consulting, getting a commercial real estate broker's license which I have used and benefited from for the last forty years, and a move to LA into filmmaking. Life for everyone is made up of decisions, non-decisions, paths both taken and not taken. We only have one go around, so it would be shameful to miss any of what life has to offer.

This book is intended to be uplifting, giving me and those who read it a greater enthusiasm for living a good pleasure-filled life. Death is easy; it's living that's hard, but the rewards of life are plenty. It's not that life is so short that drives me to make the most of it, but because death is so long.

The End

38122603R00124

Made in the USA
San Bernardino, CA
06 June 2019